Kink and the City

(An Englishman in New York)

First Edition

Published by The Nazca Plains Corporation
Las Vegas, Nevada
2010

ISBN: 978-1-61098-110-1
Ebook: 978-1-61098-111-8

Published by

The Nazca Plains Corporation ®
4640 Paradise Rd, Suite 141
Las Vegas NV 89109-8000

Cover Photo, Songquan Deng
Art Director, Blake Stephens

Dedication

For my Mother…who would have been totally appalled by this.

Kink and the City

(An Englishman in New York)

First Edition

John Smith

Contents

Preface

Look…if you've picked up this book in the hope of simply reading about salacious kink oriented experiences and to satiate your own base desires well, in all honesty, you've probably come to the right place…because that's really what this book is about. The title says it all. It's an account of an occasionally amiable Englishman arriving in New York and attempting to re discover his fetish roots after a long hiatus…and meeting the best and the worst this subculture has to offer (for indeed it is a subculture).

No I'm not going to attempt to either vindicate myself or pass judgement on others (much as I'd dearly love to), but I'll be as honest as I can. You'll understand that probity and good English manners prevent me from using real names and the characters I describe are of course disguised but, and this is key, everything I've described here is real. And, unlike many similar narratives, I've most certainly not stolen other people's stories as my own! Being involved in kink is a lot like being involved with a model car racing club. Yes, you did read that correctly. Let me explain.

Model car racing clubs are a haven for those individuals who like such marginal activities. They join to be surrounded by like-minded people and rejoice in the fact they can talk about their unique obsessions in a non-judgmental and non-threatening environment. As a spotty twelve year old (and an obsessive model car racing freak) I recall rubbing my hands in anticipation the day the BBC announced an hours documentary on the subject. Hey, what can I say? In my defence I was young!

It came as something of a shock to my naïve sensibilities when it was revealed these enclaves were almost exclusively the domain of obsessive overweight middle aged men with no lives. Men seeking approval and perceived respect in a pecking order amongst similarly challenged overweight middle-aged men with the same aspirations. Equally there were the intricate politics, petty needs and jealousies which go with such a scenario. Kink can be a lot like that, especially the 'obsessive overweight middle aged men' part. I guess the main difference between the two worlds is there's generally a lot more nudity in kink circles than there is in the model car racing world…which I think we should be very thankful for… at least most of the time.

Kinksters are just like anyone else except for the fact they're kinky. There's the mediocre, the bad, the indifferent and the just plain awful. Equally there's the bright, the beautiful, the skilful and the very best of the best. For every 'Mistress Halitosis' and 'Master Enormous', there's a…well we'll talk about the real stars a little later…but they're out there…burning bright in the fetish firmament.

Arriving in Manhattan to put my roots down I was about to discover this. In fact, I was about to discover rather a lot.

Chapter One

Roots

Spanking. There, have I got your attention? Google it and you'll come up with a staggering seventeen million pages on the subject...no matter what you may think, this is not a minority interest. If you've never been spanked but have fantasized about it you may feel you've missed out. Indeed you have. You've missed out on the fact it bloody hurts. An element which often comes as an unwelcome shock to a first time player. Far better to be a 'Top' (someone who enjoys spanking people) as opposed to a 'bottom' (a recipient).

The cross I bear, which, sadly, is one of a very great many, is that I'm a 'switch'. That's someone who enjoys both topping and bottoming. The phrase 'enjoys bottoming' is something of an exaggeration. For some inexplicable reason the need to experience it builds up in me to a stage where I have to satiate the desire. On a run up to such a scene I fantasise about all aspects of what's to come but I don't fantasise about the pain because the body doesn't really remember it.

By the time the scenario is in play I'm lapping up all the mouth watering preamble right up to the moment of 'first contact', i.e. the first strike. Then my internal reaction is, 'Omigawd, what the bloody hell was I thinking?' And it's the same every time and yet I keep going back for more. No, I don't understand either…but it's delicious…honestly. I approach the activity with the enthusiasm of a proctologist with a glove puppet fetish watching the Muppets.

Which brings me to 'Roots'. The title of this chapter. How did I get started? Was I abused as a child? No. Was I beaten by an attractive woman at school? Sadly no, I wasn't even beaten by an unattractive woman. Was I from a broken home? No. Have I had drug problems? No, I could always afford them. So, having established I was evidently born with my eclectic proclivities and not had them foisted upon me, the next question has to be, "Where did it all go right?"

Kink entered my life early. It was back in the balmy halcyon days when my main interests were steam trains and stamp collecting. Little did I know my obscenely healthy thoughts regarding these harmless activities were about to be pushed to the back of my modest cerebral processes. The catalyst was my classmate Susan.

I can still recall the moment sat in the school playground. Two eight year olds eating their lunches ruminating on life's rich mosaic when she offered, with no preamble whatsoever, that she fantasised about spanking on a regular basis. Almost choking on my apple I pressed her for more information which resulted in my listening, almost hypnotized, for the next thirty minutes as she reeled off the various scenarios that intrigued her.

After hearing what she had to say they now intrigued me too. They intrigued me a lot. In fact they intrigued me far more than anything ever had before. By the time she'd finished her discourse, steam trains and postage stamps were but a misty memory and, thank God, they still are.

Susan too is now a misty memory, but I wonder if it hadn't been for her lighting that fire if I'd be different today. Maybe that fire was already built and just needed her to light it or perhaps in that half hour she both built and lit it. Finer minds than mine (and I'm continually assured there are a great many) have pondered this question with no real conclusion.

From that moment onwards I feverishly sought out and devoured all the available literature on the subject. Unfortunately 'all the available literature on the subject' for an eight year old in England in the sixties consisted of the odd reference in otherwise numbingly dull books. Certainly there was a colourful Ice lolly available at the time called 'Kinky' (yes really) and a brand of Ice Cream called 'Mr Whippy', both amusing references naturally lost on me at that tender age. Nonetheless I consumed whatever I was able to find with rapt enthusiasm whilst wrongly cogitating on the fact that both Susan and I were obviously pretty unique in our interests. Mind you, at eight years old, I also thought erections were something which only happened to me, an occurrence that gave me sleepless nights fearing discovery of my apparently freakishly renegade appendage.

Eventually I went through the rite of passage that was de rigueur for English boys. I swapped my short trousers for long ones and secured a paper route. Waiting for my papers one day I was, as usual, discreetly scanning the top shelf magazines when I came across one exclusively devoted to spanking. My chest tightened and my heartbeat went through the roof. I was not alone! And not only that, they actually published magazines about this stuff! This was a revelation of almost biblical proportions.

My peer group talked constantly about the stress of sneaking their regular girlie magazines past their parents into their homes. I could only dream of such luxury. The thought of being caught bringing spanking magazines into the house… well…it's probably why I can deal with stress and pressure so well today. I eventually made it to sixteen without being found out and took the decision to vacate the tissue mountain that was my bedroom and leave home to seek my fortune.

There is a philosophy which says like attracts and we draw things to ourselves. Why am I mentioning this? Well, I rented a room from Stacy, a most attractive woman in her middle thirties. She was funny and direct. She was also, unbeknownst to me at the time, a professional dominatrix.

Chapter Two

Lift off

Stacy was a force of nature. Quite how much of a force of nature however I was yet to fully appreciate. Whilst I furtively inhabited a modest room on the upper floor of her house I would hear her having incredibly long conversations on the telephone, the details of which were impossible to make out through the walls. I'd never known anyone spend so much time on the phone. She also had two lines which I'd never even heard of in a private house. I'd also never known anyone have such a large amount of mail.

Though curious I kept my own counsel and in return she was a gracious landlady, never intrusive, always apparently happy and possessed of the oddest set of business hours I'd ever seen. Sometimes I knew she'd been at home all day. Sometimes she'd vanish in the evening saying she was 'off to do some work'. I mentioned this to a parent of a friend. He'd chuckled and offered the opinion that she could be 'on the game' at the 'high class end'.

Despite still being relatively naïve I discounted this as an option due to what she wore went she went striding off. Flat shoes, jeans, regular jacket etc. As time went by we came to know each other better. She'd been places and done things that I could only yet dream of and I found her fascinating. In turn she seemed to genuinely enjoy having a callow youth around, albeit a well-behaved and respectful one. In a few months a friendship developed, a friendship helped by the fact that I was not immune to her very striking feminine charms.

The nadir came one evening when we were sitting around sipping Chardonnay and chatting. She could take her drink but I was sixteen with a tolerance for wine which would have made a lab rat's capacity look like hardened alcoholism. After three glasses I would have confessed anything to anyone about anything. In that moment of fermented grape induced bonhomie I blurted out, "What exactly is it that you do for a living?" Without a moments hesitation she replied, "I'm a professional dominatrix."

I had no idea what that was. I'd never even heard the expression. My sole kink exposure to date having been a few tame spanking magazines and a playground conversation some eight years previously. No Internet to educate in those far off days. Kinksters today don't know how lucky they are and I've just realised with a cringe that I sound like my parents.

"What's that?" I slurred engagingly.

She laughed and delved into a draw in a nearby cabinet. A moment later she was sitting back down flipping through a magazine she'd retrieved. She stopped at a page and handed it to me. "This is my business," she offered.

I think I must have literally resembled a cartoon character at that point insomuch as I'll swear my jaw actually dropped to the ground. There was Stacy in all her glory, that glory being her alter ego 'Mistress Alexandra' who was evidently both 'Cruel and demanding'; at least that's what it said. It also warned that 'Savage beatings' could be expected as could 'Traditional discipline' together with something called 'Genitorture' which I didn't like the sound of at all. Mistress Alexandra's lithe body, encompassed in leather, replete with incredibly high boots, stared back at me from the page with pursed lips and an inquiring raised eyebrow. Her eyebrow wasn't the only thing raised, I had never seen anything so sexy.

I seriously doubt if anyone reading this needs to be told what a Dominatrix is, and frankly, if you do, it's probably way past your bedtime so I'll not detail the obvious. The next hour (and a few more glasses of Chardonnay later) I was fully briefed. Briefed and excited. In those pre Internet days she advertised mainly through the 'scene magazine' which she'd shown me, hence the second phone line. The bulk of her PR was undertaken through contact magazines explaining the unusually large mail drop. I was agog with fascination. She was just like me! Yes, I really was that young and stupid! I poured myself yet another glass of wine.

Whilst nursing a hangover of gargantuan proportions the following day I couldn't shake these revelations from my head. Men actually paid women to beat them. I'd never imagined such a thing. The evidence also suggested they paid women to do a great deal more than just that. Additionally, my reproductive equipment had been resonating like castanets upon seeing Stacy's outfit. It made me think/want all sorts of things, things I'd never thought of or even considered before. Until that moment fetish for me was imagining myself spanking or caning a recalcitrant schoolgirl. Clearly this kink thing was a much broader church than I'd ever considered. It demanded further enquiry, enquiries I was prepared to make vigorously.

It didn't take long to find out more. The following evening Stacy strode in, the first words out of her mouth being, "So you're into spanking eh?" I flushed crimson. Further interrogation revealed in the latter part of the previous evening I'd hinted at my own proclivities under alcohols tender prompting. Now, stone cold sober, I was mortally embarrassed, an embarrassment that my landlady with a clearly relished delight, rode over like General Patton advancing on Berlin. An hour later I had no secrets...none.

The following week she took me to her place of work. An innocuous looking house in the leafy suburbs of North London it contained three large bedrooms equipped for the job of professional domination, a further bedroom served as a repository for the various Dommes outfits. The whole place was a kinkster's paradise. I looked aghast yet felt myself strangely thrilled by the whips and floggers hung on the walls. I murmured approval at the vast array of canes, straps and assorted beating paraphernalia. I feigned indifference at the intricate bondage devices on display whilst disguising my intense curiosity. I was also genuinely appalled by some pieces which Stacy informed me were for 'Genitorture'. These days it's called 'CBT' or for the uninitiated, cock and ball torture. I felt my own genitals shrink to the size something very small indeed and moved on. I was just an old-fashioned spanker... wasn't I?

Actually, though I thought of myself as such, thinking was all I was doing at that point. Little did I know that I wouldn't get the chance to deal with my first pert upturned derrière for almost a decade. For now I was just delighted to simply be in the company of someone who understood, someone who understood a great deal more than I did.

Stacy had no salacious story to tell per se so don't get your hopes up. An apparently straight arrow university graduate from a good home with loving parents, she'd sought out fetish parties in her early twenties. After a number of conversations with kink professionals and some serious soul searching she'd given up her well-paid job in the city to thrash people in the suburbs. For the most part she actually enjoyed her work and she certainly enjoyed the abundant tax-free cash and the flexible hours. Her wicked sense of humour helped her deal with some of the less than savoury requests she received (of which there were a great many) and her intelligence enabled her to keep a healthy distance from her clients.

Her kink roots? Seeing a Wonder Woman comic in her early teens. For her, a life changer. Her revelation reminded me as a kid I did pay extra attention to the TV when Catwoman was featured on Batman. Catwoman made me feel something but I wasn't quite sure what it was. Julie Newmar has a lot to answer for.

To say my landlady opened my eyes is a gross understatement. We often sat reading her mail together critiquing the spelling and sniggering at the grammar. I can recall reading some of the epistles with eyes like saucers, sometimes simply agog at the complexity of the requests and, sadly, sometimes nauseated. Bad syntax can have that effect and so can perverts though being one myself I learned to be tolerant. She taught me the rudiments of the single tail whip, making me practice on a tailors dummy for hours on end, a grounding that proved most useful when I eventually learned the finer points from New York's top practitioner, a master class indeed.

Stacy and I developed a unique relationship despite our twenty-year age difference which seemed enormous at the time. We became friends, a friendship that occasionally, when the planets lined up, was intimate. She was a free spirit. A dated term now but she defined it. She personified rampaging hedonism and taught me to embrace it as enthusiastically as she did.

She laughingly once told me she insisted on having her medical matters dealt with by an eighty year old gynaecologist because his hand shook. I think she was only half joking. Some women's sexuality is as subtle as the hint of lavender on a warm summer breeze. Stacy's was like a raging forest fire that torched everything in its path.

Prior to meeting her my own sexual history had reached the dizzy heights of finally loosing my virginity a few months previously. The venue was Crete and was linked to a robust initiation to Ouzo. The details are relatively hazy now but I do recall mumbling a most inappropriate suggestion to a woman considerably older than me who stunned me by immediately agreeing. Struck dumb by a combination of her acquiescence and a huge amount of imbibed alcohol, she practically force marched me to a moonlit beach and demanded I make good my intentions. To this day I have ineffably fond memories and heartfelt thanks for her forbearance. I am also delighted to report that I have subsequently managed to avoid the combination of physical union and sand ever again.

Stacy helped refine my technique. A sixteen year olds propensity to go stampeding towards the clitoris at the first hint of intimacy needs to be reined in early. Err I'm speaking talking generally of course. I certainly wasn't referring to me you understand!

A year later my circumstances changed and I left, educated in a way my parents certainly wouldn't have approved of but I have no regrets save one. On a number of occasions Stacy enquired if I'd like to play with her. Each time I fled like a frightened rabbit, thinking of myself purely as a 'top'. She never tried to push me and now I grind my teeth that I declined. I was too inexperienced and immature to realise I could enjoy submitting to someone genuinely worth submitting to. It is one of my few lasting regrets. I did once generously offer to spank her, an offer which was met with a dark chuckle and a stare that would have felled a fully-grown African bull elephant at five thousand paces.

Thinking I could now embrace the kink side of my persona I began my new life only to find in those pre Internet days it was almost impossible. For the next ten years, as far as kink was concerned, I felt like a wheelchair bound man at a basketball game. i.e. relatively close to the action but unlikely to score.

Chapter Three

Back in the Saddle

I gazed lazily out of the plane window and watched the lights of Hong Kong fall behind me. The United States was God knows how many hours away and I was suffering the wretched depravations of economy class. Despite the discomfort I had a warm glow as I reflected on the previous two days spent in the company of a hard core submissive. Anouk was one hundred and five pounds of roller coaster masochistic enthusiasm and to her (and my) delight I'd beaten and whipped her mercilessly.

I was en route home to Manhattan, where I'd settled four years previously to start anew and to re embrace that which I'd unexpectedly denied myself for so long.

In my mid twenties I started a relationship with a woman who not only shared my own proclivities but who's desires and sensuous creativity often left me, literally and figuratively, gasping for breath. During that time we and the many friends we made in the scene drank deeply from the kink and 'erotic activities' cups. We delighted in and celebrated our sexuality and wicked inclinations with very few limits. Scarcely any stones had been left unturned in our boundary pushing expeditions into unbridled hedonism. A few weeks into our relationship some drunken pillow talk had revealed a mutual interest in 'matters eclectic'. From that moment it was like two greyhounds exiting their traps as the electric rabbit swept past, except for the fact that we'd have probably beaten the greyhounds to the finish line…in reality we'd have probably caught the rabbit! A friend once wistfully remarked, "Debauchery is underrated." Well, not by us it wasn't.

But that relationship is not what this book is about. After fifteen outstanding and eventful years together life's circumstances changed and we parted company. Business dictated I move to Mainland Europe where I spent eight long and totally wretched years surrounded by blasted foreigners trying to pretend I wasn't kinky. Opportunities to play in countries where English wasn't the first language posed insurmountable problems. Why didn't I just learn the language you may ask? Well, being British I naturally have a calm easy distain for such things; totally unconscionable but sadly true. I like to think that my indifference is maintaining at least some sort of international standardization. The extent of my communication with the locals largely consisted of me shouting at them in English when they failed to understand me. Yes, I'm truly shamed.

Thankfully life's vagaries once again conspired to re locate me and Gotham had beckoned, whispering encouragingly like a distant mistress. Despite the onset of middle age delivering the threat of an expanding waistline and a significantly receding hairline I resolved to get back into to the kink saddle when I arrived. Now, four years later, I'd most certainly done so, in fact if anything I was now a little saddle sore. With Anouks squealing still fresh in my mind I was returning home to New York from a brief business trip to Hong Kong. I was flying in via Boston to deal with 'Pernicious Penny', then onto Chicago to take care of 'Juiced Jeanine'. The night after I arrived back in the city I was to give 'Hard Core Hanna' her just desserts. Not only was I saddle sore, frankly I was chafing a little as well. A far cry from when I first arrived in the city.

I initially settled into an exceedingly modest abode on the Upper West Side. I had considered the Upper East Side but the thought of being the only person without a face lift was unappealing. I longed to live in the Village or Soho but I'd missed my window both age and cash wise. I consoled myself that John Lennon had lived on the West Side and though it hadn't turned out too well for him my profile was a mite lower so I thought I'd take the risk. The five story walk up had been an ambitious choice but cognisant that my 'racing snake' physique was being challenged by advancing years, I thought the exercise would do me good.

I resolved to take my time finding out about the scene, suppressing my natural inclination to charge in like an angry Rhinoceros on amphetamines. The reality was the moment the Timer Warner internet installation man had finished his work I practically pushed him out of the door so I could furiously tap away online.

I've indicated that spankings my thing but over the years my tastes broadened a little. The first revelation when I actually started playing back in the day was if I 'believed' in the top I could also very occasionally 'bottom'. Domestic scenes of spanking and caning developed through to flogger and horsewhip scenes. Restraints then followed (how else to keep someone still for a single tail whip?) and, on occasion, the odd torture session to keep things interesting. Though broadened, my pursuits still centred around discipline and punishment. Not being a senior member of the clergy the thought of being buggered senseless by a strap-on wielding harridan didn't float my boat. Dressing up as a woman held no appeal as I wasn't an English high court judge and being trussed up like an Xmas Turkey with an orange stuffed in my mouth didn't work as I wasn't a well known politician. Needles and piercing were a no no because I'm not clinically insane and so it goes on…and I'm just scratching the surface here. Hey, it's all good (so I'm told), but I know what I like.

What the Americans call 'Corporal' was my penchant so I needed to find someone to spank. How does one find such an individual? Believe it or not I simply Googled 'Spankee Manhattan' and, incredibly, an entry on Craigslist popped up. I double clicked and was drawn to a listing featuring a photograph of one of the most pert rear ends I'd ever seen. The verbiage related that the woman concerned was prepared to fess up for a fee and took great pains to emphasise she was not interested in any other activity. Short, sweet and to the point. The thought of paying had never even occurred to me but her bottom looked wonderful and I was impatient.

I stroked my chin thoughtfully (actually I didn't but I thought it would make the narrative seem more realistic) and considered what I had read. Surely, if the picture was real this woman must be snowed under with business? Equally I'd never 'paid to play' but I was eager to get going so I had no problem putting my hand in my pocket to kick things off. I tapped out a note which essentially said, 'Are you for real?' A minute or so later a rather sharply written missive arrived indicating she was indeed for real and she had no truck whatsoever with timewasters. Suitably chastened I entered into a brief email exchange, the results of which had me slinking off to her apartment that very afternoon feverish with anticipation.

On my journey downtown I was actually nervous. I hadn't played for so long I had to dig deep to mine my 'top' persona. Even though I was a paying customer I wanted to give the best impression. There's nothing worse than a nervous top (or as we refer to them within kink circles, dickheads).

Standing outside her door I was about to press the bell when I was taken aback by the sounds of what was most definitely a comprehensive spanking taking place within. I checked my watch. I was on time. Clearly her previous customer must still be with her. I cringed thinking what her poor rear must look like after taking what were evidently dawn till dusk thrashings on a daily basis. I mooched unhappily back onto the street and walked around the block looking in vain for a Starbucks. Jesus, the East Village had changed. I recall a time when I wouldn't have driven through the place in a tank even if I'd had an escort from a full team of Airborne Rangers. It was now almost twee.

Ten minutes later my cell phone trilled. 'Committed Chloe' (as she came to be known) enquired as to why I was late. Before I could get a word in edgeways I was told I'd better be there soon and with that she hung up. I scurried back to her abode whilst ruminating upon the fact that I was supposed to be the dominant one.

All was made clear once I'd set foot across the threshold. A stunning Blue and Yellow Macaw and a feisty Amazon parrot ruled the roost, their mimicking abilities reflecting life and activity in the apartment. To this day it's one of the most hilarious things I've ever witnessed. Squeals, belt strokes, scolding...nothing was beyond these birds verbal range.

Chloe was an exceeding pretty woman in her mid twenties with the body of a teenage girl. Perfect. She was also, I was to find out, a hard wired 'spankhead' of laudable commitment to the cause. She greeted me politely, explained the rules (i.e. nothing sexual), showed me her collection of implements and asked me what I wanted to do. "That is for me to know and you to find out young lady," I replied brusquely and handed her the required payment. The moment the words were out of my mouth I knew my nervousness had been misplaced. I asked her about her 'safe word' to which she sniffed, "I won't need one." For the uninitiated a 'safe word' is a pre agreed word used when a recipient has had enough or wants to stop or ease up for a moment. I personally didn't like playing with one as it gives control back to the bottom. The fail safe I prefer to play with (for there has to be one) is if a sub says 'stop' then that's it, session over. That makes them think twice about blurting it out.

I placed a chair into the centre of the room, pulled her over to me whilst undoing the top button of her jeans. With a quick downward motion I unzipped her and with one deft tug her trousers and panties were down by her ankles. I chastised her for her attitude on the phone and the poor quality of her implement collection. I then motioned her over my knees and started with baby slaps on her perfect butt.

I began building up the pace and intensity whilst watching her reactions carefully. Quality play is about balance and limits. Even though she'd taken hard cash for what she was receiving she deserved to know (as indeed do all 'bottoms') she was playing with someone to whom her welfare was paramount. I needn't have worried. My charge sucked up an increasingly hard hand spanking with barely a twitch. It was only by the time I slipped into third gear some ten minutes later that that some modest squirming occurred. The heavy breathing didn't start until I was whaling her almost as hard as I could. The heavy breathing was mine…it was exhausting!

Mopping my brow I stood her up and noticed just the very hint of a smirk on her face. Feigning annoyance I had her bend over a chair whilst I removed my heavy leather belt with a theatrical flourish. Thirty-six full force strokes removed any semblance of the aforesaid smirk. Now it was her who was breathing heavily. With the parrots squawking enthusiastically I pushed my advantage. I laid her over the chair with her hands on the floor and proceeded to give her rapid strokes with a lightweight paddle. I knew by now I was dealing with a true aficionado. And so it went on, multiple positions and implements for the next twenty or so minutes.

"We're done," I declared after the final stroke of the fraternity paddle had been delivered. Chloe removed her hands from her knees and stood up. "Jesus," she breathed "That was a challenge!" I grinned back at her, basking in the knowledge that finally, after my wilderness years, I was back.

At least that's what I thought…

Chapter Four

Next Steps

Chloe was a mine of information when it came to spanking and New York. I thought I was an early starter finding my persuasions at eight years old but she beat me by a full four years. She also stunned me by admitting at twenty one she'd gone out and actually paid a woman to give her her first spanking. Now that's real dedication! I was respect personified. Unprompted, she regaled me with the most colourful stories of her clientele. Whilst she was very discreet about identity she certainly wasn't about their shortcomings as disciplinarians. I rubbed my hands together in delight as their various inadequacies were listed until I realised that I may well be next on the list. She took no prisoners whatsoever.

There was the three hundred pound guy who, by the time he'd climbed the stairs to her apartment was too exhausted to deal with her. There was 'Mr Soft Spanker' who, literally, on one occasion had put her to sleep over his knee. One of my favourites was a 'gentleman' who'd conducted a session with her and asked if on the next occasion she would come to his place and consent to being sealed in a cardboard box! This was a new one on me. I'd read that doing something imaginative with a feather is erotic. It's when you do something with the whole chicken its perversion. I don't know quite where cardboard boxes fit into the equation. It was certainly a long list of war stories. War stories that I liked as they showed Chloe to be the very type of no nonsense aficionado that I enjoy playing with the most when topping.

The people in kink have many labels. Enormously tedious amounts have been written about this and I'm not going to enter into a tiresome monologue debating the pros and cons of the arguments here. Chloe was very much like I am when I bottom. I submit but I'm not submissive. There's a huge distinction here between us and true submissives insomuch as they…oops…nearly did it…felt a tiresome monologue coming on and just stopped it in time.

Chloe was like me insomuch as the right to top her has got to be earned. She too was disdainful of wannabes and those who assume an implement in their hands or looking good in leather equals dominance. Wrong! We could both spot a rubbish top half a mile away through thick fog whilst wearing a blindfold. It's in the demeanour, the tone of voice and the look. If you're a 'submitter' a real Top can silence you across a crowded room with the raise of an eyebrow. You've either 'got it' or you ain't. All this is totally irrelevant to a true submissive as most of them would bottom to a can of beans if it was wrapped in leather… and fair enough. As for slaves, well we really don't have the time to go there. No offence to slaves intended…we're all floating our boats in the same water.

Equally she really 'got' this stuff. Domestic discipline is about ritual, positioning, atmosphere, cold silences, shame and embarrassment. It's a visit to the headmaster's office or the cruel Aunt or best of all (at least for me) the strict Governess. If you're going do these scenes then try to do them properly. Sure it's pretend but the shock of the pain isn't. If that's real then attention to the ancillaries should be undertaken in an equally committed fashion. The really best scenes have all these components. It takes practice. We all started somewhere.

Chloe's gig was exclusively 'domestic discipline'. Not for her the accoutrements of the dungeon and whips and floggers. 'Domestic' is very much a niche within a niche and those participants tend to keep to their boundaries with a passion. I understood those boundaries as they used to be my own and respected them accordingly.

On my way home I ruminated on her sadly deficient selection of implements. Deficient it may have been but it was significantly superior to mine as I had none whatsoever save for an old single tail whip that I'd had for years. I knew I could go online but with a further visit booked with Chloe in a week time was not on my side. I called her asking for guidance.

She gave me the name and address of what was apparently the best place to buy spanking implements in the city. Though I trusted her judgement I didn't feel entirely comfortable with her suggestion.

It was a store called 'The Leatherman'.

Accordingly, a little later, I emerged from the subway and made my way up Christopher Street. The West Village had undoubtedly retained its inherent gayness despite Manhattans overall gentrification. It's still a great place to take a stroll no matter what your sexuality. Upon seeing the shop on the opposite side of the road I immediately froze. Red faced I turned my back and stared intently into the window of the store beside me. If I'd arrived a minute earlier disaster would have been the order of the day. A good friend was exiting the store with two friends in tow and a bag filled with God knows what under his arm. I knew Mark was gay, indeed it was difficult to conclude otherwise however I didn't know he was kinky and he most certainly didn't know I was. A circumspect manner and discretion were not within his purview.

He wore his gayness not like a badge but as a neon coloured sign illuminated by industrial strength arc lights. If someone wants to bowl from the pavilion end then that's their prerogative and Mark certainly luxuriated in his persuasion. He was more camp than a whole field of tents, mortifyingly indiscreet, outrageously insensitive…and yet hugely intelligent and creative. He revelled in his pathological promiscuity. It's said that women generally need to have a reason to have sex whereas most men just need a place…Mark even re writes those rules but I can't fault him for his total enthusiasm in such matters. Having said that I'd really prefer not to be privy to the grim details which he revealed endlessly with lascivious enthusiasm.

Despite these predilections I enjoyed my encounters with him. Normally in an all male gathering one is expected to talk about sport. Not me. As far as I'm concerned, when it comes to sport, a 'pinch hitter' is a piece of emergency equipment found on a Lobster boat, a 'draft pick' is selecting what hole to plug when you've got a limited amount of filler and as for a 'double header', you really don't want to know what I thought that might be. These subjects never arise when Marks about…I never know what he's going to say next and that's the pleasure in knowing him.

I filed away my knowledge of his newly discovered additional quirk and, after he'd disappeared off down the street, with some trepidation I slunk covertly into Leatherman.

Chapter Five

Accoutrements etc

As I pushed open the door of the establishment I realised that I'd forgotten the T-shirt that I normally wear when around gay men. The shirt bears the legend *'Err actually I'm not gay'*. Nonetheless I took a deep breath and stepped inside. Behind the cash desk was an enormous leather clad tattooed biker type with wrists like my thighs and biceps like the Goodyear blimp. "Hi," he offered brightly, "What are you looking for?" "Implements," I stuttered in my best 'Err actually I'm not gay' voice. He motioned to a spiral staircase leading downstairs… no doubt leading to 'straight hell' itself.

I eased past a display positively groaning with bottomless leather chaps and made my way down the stairway fully expecting to be greeted the Devil himself. As I reached the bottom I was confronted by quite the largest selection of dildos I'd ever seen. I was astonished at their sheer scale. Even with my lack of imagination I knew what the 'final destination' of these things was and frankly some of them looked a mite ambitious for the purpose. I'd heard stories from Mark that some gays occasionally took relaxants to help them accommodate the serious stuff. Judging by the gargantuan monster at the end of the display they should have been selling it with a supply of horse tranquilisers! It was about this time I suddenly wondered what level of reality I was supposed to be relating to.

Affecting an air of studied nonchalance I continued past a wall featuring a veritable smorgasbord of devices devoted solely to the infliction of pain on male genetalia. Metal gleamed and leather shone in a celebration of creativity and design. If you wanted your crown jewels crushed, spiked, twisted, bound up or electrocuted you really couldn't go wrong. I marvelled at their ingenuity, shuddered to the depths of my soul and moved on past the 'Sounds' display until I reached the implement section.

'Sounds'? It was a puzzler for me as well until I saw the explanation on a display box. Stainless steel rods in various sizes inserted into the end of ones penis. No, I didn't get it either, and, call me old fashioned, I hoped I never did. I've subsequently been informed that I didn't know what I was missing. I'll take the risk it's one of life's experiences that I'll forgo without regret.

I'm elitist about implements, very elitist indeed. If we're talking dungeon play then for me that's about quality floggers and single tail whips made by people who actually know what they're doing and care about their work. It's absolutely worth the time to seek out the good stuff. If you really care about your kink, do your research. You'll be so glad you did. If we're talking 'domestic' then canes, tawses, straps, paddles and hairbrushes are the order of the day. Nothing made of plastic and certainly nothing in exotic colours and absolutely nothing that smacks of 'fun' (if you'll excuse the pun). In my humble opinion, in the same way that there's no such thing as a 'fun run', there's also no such thing as a 'fun spanking'. It's an oxymoron, a bit like 'Cricket Highlights' on the BBC.

For the uninitiated, a single tail whip is, well, a whip obviously. Think Indiana Jones type whip but shorter. Single tails can reach up to eight feet long or more for the terminally excessive but in reality an average length of four foot works best. It's a usable size, yet is long enough to be able to demonstrate some theatricality. A bullwhip? It's just a single tail with a rigid handle. I say 'just a single tail'. In reality the single tail is at the peak of mount Olympus in terms of severity and takes serious skill to be used properly, a skill that very few people actually possess. In experienced hands it can give you the lightest stinging kiss or lay you open to the bone. In inexperienced hands…well, just don't is all I can say. You've been warned.

A flogger is like that old naval rascal, the cat o nine tails. The difference being that a flogger can have between nine to thirty six tails and these tails are made generally from leather strips and can range between twelve to twenty four inches long. The thickness of the strips and the weight and type of leather used determine the severity. They feel 'thuddy' when applied. The lighter ones are more for theatre whilst the heavy ones can ruin your day…or your entire week.

A tawse is a contrivance that originated way back in misty highlands of bonnie Scotland. I don't know why I'm being so bloody romantic about it, it's a bastard of an implement, the most classic of all being the Lochgelly, which is still produced by the original company of the same name. It's a leather strap eighteen to twenty four inches long, up to an inch and a half wide and around a quarter of an inch thick. It's split down the middle to a depth of around six to eight inches. Once again, as with a flogger, it comes in various weights. These suckers smart like crazy, like being hit with leather belt but heavier.

A strap is normally a strip of leather or rubber anything from twelve to twenty four inches long. They can start at an inch wide and go up to as much as four inches and be up to quarter of an inch thick for the really severe examples. The strap is fastened to a wooden handle. The design variants are almost infinite. Think old-fashioned barbers strop with a handle without the accompanying nauseating cherub cheeked close harmony quartet. These guys are the 'Kings of Sting'. The lighter ones simply feel unpleasant whilst the heavy versions bring on what can only be described as 'white pain'…especially the rubber variety.

A paddle is self-explanatory and if you need me to tell you what a hairbrush is then you need to take a very close look at your life.

The Leatherman serviced some of my needs most effectively. Their selection of straps and paddles was exemplary. Their floggers in the main were most certainly serviceable and their single tails, whilst not of the finest quality, represented a good entry point for the newbie. Sadly, as is oddly the norm with most kink retailers, their canes were woefully below par.

The cane is generally the most feared weapon in a domestic disciplinarians arsenal, especially amongst many Americans who have no cultural associations with it. It was a constant source of amazement to find that even amongst some of the very serious domestic players I eventually came across, this was the one implement that they'd eschewed up to the point of meeting me. I put thing's right of course. After all it would have been rude not to. Subsequently these very people were the ones who became its most serious devotees.

Why it's the most feared I think is its imagery. The archetypal Headmaster or stern Governess bending a cane theatrically in front of the trembling supplicant. The sound it makes and of course the anticipation of the pain it'll cause. Yes it does hurt and yes it can be very severe but it has a sublime elegance unmatched by other items. I've been hit so hard with a paddle it's made my teeth rattle and almost knocked my contact lenses out but it's only when my tormenter brings out the cane my blood really runs cold. It's also the domestic implement that takes the most practice to use safely. This isn't a 'how to' book but if you're new to it, for Gods sake practice on a cushion for accuracy. With the exception of the French, there are few things in life I find unacceptable but a lack of skill sets is certainly one.

Trying to find decent canes is a labour of love. Fortunately I knew of a husband and wife team in the UK who hit the sweet spot perfectly with their homemade offerings. A pair of committed enthusiasts who understood the finer nuances of this most dramatic of accoutrements. Three of their finest offerings were winging their way across the North Atlantic at that very moment. A 'junior', a 'senior' and a delicious 'dragon'. Unbeknownst to her, Chloe would be making their acquaintance at our next encounter.

After mooching around and swinging a few choice pieces through the air I secured a robust prison strap, two paddles of different weights and sizes, a particularly vicious tawse and a singularly unpleasant looking rubber slapper. My collection had re started.

Whilst wandering back to the subway station I came across a pharmacy. I was struck by two things. The first was a splendid display of hairbrushes in the window and the second? I was stunned to realise I'd visited this pharmacy for a very different reason almost thirty years beforehand. I recognised it as back then they also had a wonderful hairbrush display although my reason for visiting on that occasion was very different. I was a fey 21 year old, in New York for the first time.

After arriving fairly late I'd unpacked in feverish excitement and, almost breathless in anticipation, scooted downtown looking for adventure.   After frequenting a few clubs I eventually found 'adventure' and suggested my hotel room would be a better place to get further acquainted than her student accommodation.

We jumped into a cab and being the gentleman I am, I made a stop off at this very pharmacy to purchase the necessary protective gear for such a liaison. I dashed in, quickly grabbed what I needed off the counter and within ten minutes we were at the hotel.

At the appropriate time I reached over to the pack, ripped it open with a gusto, to be confronted by mint flavoured chewing gum!

Life one. Me Nil. A recurring pattern.

Misty eyed with nostalgia I walked in and secured myself a stout ebony backed hairbrush. Within a few short months my implement draw was fuller than a United Airlines complaints box.

Chapter Six

Up to Speed

A week later, awaiting Chloe's arrival, I cogitated on what had transpired since our last meeting. In amongst the plethora of information and advice she'd kindly proffered was a website where spankoholics could post threads about issues related to their kink and, more importantly, advertise for meet ups with like-minded people. Time spent on the Internet, especially investigating matters that one should be doing and not just reading about, was not a preferred way of using my time. Nonetheless, realising I'd need to take a little metaphorical pain to re establish myself I plunged in.

The threads section was a revelation. A revelation that the majority of the posters seemed to be lacking a spell-check facility on their computers and had evidently left school well before they'd mastered basic grammar. I'd never linked kink to low IQ's, indeed my experience back in the day was exactly the opposite. With a heavy heart I pushed on. Clearly the majority of posters were just talking and not doing and this site was their only link to that which they craved. I felt compassion (no, really, I did), but felt compelled to ignore their tedious whining and go straight to the 'meet up' section.

The same criteria seemed to apply in the intellectual stakes with people wanting to get together with the notable exception that 99.9% of the posters were apparently fabulously mediocre men. I think I'd reached page eleven before I saw a solitary woman's advert and it appeared that the poor thing had been deluged with enthusiastic wannabes desperate to tend to her (and their own) needs. All very depressing stuff but I tried to be positive. I cracked my knuckles, took a deep breath and wrote my own 'ad'. I forget the exact wording but it was something along these lines.

Strict Disciplinarian in Manhattan

Safe sane mature professional man is seeking true domestic discipline enthusiasts who are bored with the pretenders and demand the real thing. I put emphasis on ritual, a strong verbal component and the use of a wide range of implements.

I'm very experienced and a passionate respecter of limits. Additionally I'm possessed of a dark sense of humour which is essential in this activity etc etc

Short, brief and to the point. I wasn't looking for a partner or romance but to connect with a few like minded players eager to have some fun. I'd run the gamut of most representations of male mating rituals and as fifty beckoned I was content to enjoy the freedom of non attachment. I'd done the 'teenage boy on the prowl' thing. I'd done the twenties 'Shagging and some serious dating thing'. Fifteen years with one person meant I'd done the 'real relationship' thing and then I'd had eight years of the 'divorcee about town 'thing'. I felt I owed myself a break. I hit the 'post' button and naively waited for my email box to fill up. Actually I wasn't that naïve but I thought I may find a diamond in the rough. A week later I'd found plenty of 'rough' but certainly no diamonds. Eleven responses...all from men, including a guy who wanted to know if I was into 'diapers'. Jesus, try reading that over breakfast!

Judging by the evident cerebral standard of most of the posters I concluded it was my fault as I hadn't been clear enough. I re posted the same 'ad' and added in capitals ABSOLUTELY NO MEN. I thought for a moment and then added. DYXLEXIA IS NO EXCUSE. The responses, such as they were, came to a grinding halt with the exception of 'diaper boy' who inexplicably came back for a second bite.

Undeterred, I put a brave face on things. I whistled happily to myself whilst I prepared the bedroom for Chloe's appointment. I carefully laid all the implements on a low table by the door (good theatre), put a ceremonial chair in the middle of the room with a cane on it and opened a new box of tissues in case of tears. With that I walked out to check my computer for the twenty seventh time that day for any further responses. There were none.

Having discussed 'matters eclectic' in great depth with Chloe at our previous meeting I knew her to be a most experienced recipient, indeed the level of her commitment to the cause had quite shocked me. Though she earned a modest sum occasionally for bottoming professionally it most certainly wasn't her main source of income. The majority of her play had been private; indeed she'd even once taken a plane to Europe simply to get a thrashing! In her early twenties, after she'd sought out and paid for her first chastisement, she'd been to all manner of play parties and clubs. Public play is not my thing but I admired her. Turning up alone as a woman to such events takes genuine courage...unless of course you actually like obsessive overweight middle aged men.

She was also hard-core, she could take it, indeed she was proud to report as much and I knew that this was said almost as a challenge. A challenge that I was up to. I knew about her experience, she didn't know very much about mine...but she was going to find out very shortly.

Topping an experienced bottom is always fun. An experienced bottom has seen/heard it all. The key to 'getting' them i.e. making them realise that they're not in control and that the top is taking them places they haven't been, is to create tension and uncertainty. This, if undertaken effectively, results in nervousness and this is what the 'bottom' is generally seeking, to be truly dominated. Not in a boots and whip way but in a more 'Oh God, what have I got myself into?' way. Even when they know that the top is both safe and sane it can be unnerving and very real. Chloe was one of those people who craved such play.

I'd set it up that for every minute late she arrived she'd get a full force stroke of an implement of my choosing on the bare with no warm up spanking. She giggled at the idea and said she'd probably arrive a couple of minutes late just for the sheer hell of it. I said nothing. She'd only played with me once so far and was in for a steep learning curve...a very steep learning curve indeed.

I was snapped from my reveries by the wind violently slamming the bedroom door shut. The force of the impact tipped the tumbler and the door locked itself from the inside. I stood in the hall aghast. It wouldn't open no matter how much I tried. All the implements and the cane were laid out neatly in the room and I'd need a locksmith to get the door open. I gulped, made the call, and sat glumly wondering how I would explain what he found when he opened the door.

While I was waiting Chloe arrived twenty minutes late genuinely apologetic. I said nothing about this transgression but brought her up to speed on the door situation. She thought it was hilarious but nevertheless we forged a plan. A short while later a ferret-faced locksmith with an Olympian class of body odour was crouched down attending to the problem. He was no doubt wondering why I was literally and figuratively breathing down his neck. The moment I heard the tumbler fall I almost physically crawled over his back to get into the room whilst Chloe distracted his attention by spontaneously offering coffee in an inordinately loud voice. It was just the hesitation I needed. In ten seconds flat everything had been swept under the bed.

Unfortunately our distraction plan necessitated us actually having coffee and chatting with the guy. We found out he had a life in the way that plankton has a life only less interesting. By the time he'd finished his drink I was close to reaching for the tissues myself as I valiantly tried to suppress my own racking sobs of boredom.

I walked Chloe into the bedroom at a leisurely pace whilst she again off handedly apologised for her lateness. I confess her lack of nervousness was admirable if somewhat misplaced. I stood her in the centre of the room with her hands on her head and reminded her of my conditions. She flushed and laughed in embarrassment. "You know," she said, "I'd genuinely forgotten about that, what with the week I've had..." Her voice tailed off as she saw I wasn't smiling. She forced an unconvincing smirk.

"You will learn to take these things seriously," I appraised her. I put her cash on the table. "Here is your fee. You were twenty minutes late so you will receive twenty strokes of one of my implements on the bare with no warm up. In addition, for forgetting my instructions you will receive a further five strokes." She wasn't smirking now; her expression was almost one of curiosity. I then reached under the bed and withdrew a cane. Her reaction was priceless. Despite her august experience it was the implement she'd always avoided. "Hey, wait a minute, you know I've never had the cane before, that's not funny," She squeaked.

"Chloe," I admonished, "You're not in control. If you want to play with me you will follow my instructions. Your fee is there on the table and it's yours to take right now whether you go through with this or not. You said you liked it 'real'; this is as real as it gets." She actually gulped bless her. "OK," she said, almost in a whisper "I'll do it."

I was enjoying myself hugely. I'd knocked her off her stride and she'd lost control of the situation and was now seriously nervous. She was a true spankhead though. Given the choice of taking the money and going, she'd taken the money and stayed. A genuine trouper…the real deal.

I motioned her to stand in front of the chair and drop her pants and underwear. Whilst she flustered around with zips and buttons I swished the cane ferociously through the air. I bent her over the chair with her palms flat on the seat. I swished the cane one more time, took a step back and paused a moment to admire her perfectly formed buttocks. I took aim, raised the cane back and delivered a stroke. The sound of the impact cut though the air like a knife. Almost immediately a lived red line appeared at the point of impact. She leapt up grabbing her butt and literally ran around in a small circle rubbing frantically. "Christ that fucking hurt," she gasped. I stared at her apparently emotionless and waited for all the fuss to die down and then put her back into position. "There's seriously no way I can take another twenty four of those," she protested.

"Right," I continued, "As you moved your hands off the chair we're going to have to start again and as you spoke without permission I'm going to add two more. That makes twenty seven to come I think." She stood bolt upright and was about to protest when she suddenly realised what she'd done. "Indeed you are correct young lady," I continued, "As you've just moved your hands off the chair yet again I'll need to add yet another two strokes. We're now up to twenty nine."

Her body language said it all. She knew that she was totally out of control and in mine. The fear for her was like fine champagne. "Remember," I reminded her, "If your hands come off the chair we go right back to stroke number one. It really doesn't matter how long this takes. I've got all afternoon." With that I stepped back and delivered stroke number two which was met with a strangled yelp. Delicious!

By stroke eight she'd still laudably held position and I was delighted to see tear droplets hitting the seat beneath her face. At stroke ten I allowed her to stand and blow her nose. She didn't talk, in fact she was speechless at that point. A cold caning for a total cane newbie is very serious stuff…especially with a dragon cane. I took the sodden tissue and put her back into position. By stroke eighteen she was in such a state I took mercy and stopped the session.

Speaking slowly I informed her, "Be aware young lady, this is the very last time I'll ever back off when we play," but she was beyond hearing at that point. I lay her on the bed and rubbed lotion into her perfectly tram lined rear. She stared into the middle distance, deep in sub space. She subsequently refused to charge me ever again for play. A humbling and rewarding accolade indeed. She got what she needed from me and I got what I needed from her. Perfect kink.

I told her about the lacklustre response to my posting. "Mention you're English," She advised. I changed the 'ad' that very evening.

The floodgates opened...well, sort of.

Chapter Seven

Dear God!

I wouldn't exactly say my cup totally overfloweth per se but upon returning home after a short business trip, to see thirteen responses to my post was certainly encouraging. Kink wise I was clearly rising like a Phoenix from the ashes. I'd neglected to remember however that Phoenix was also the name of the tutor of Achilles, who had a terminal weakness.

With ill-disguised excitement I clicked on the first letter and started to read. And I read and I read and I read. Five pages into the explicit account that were this woman's labyrinthine desires and fantasies I began to feel a little jaded. I felt even more jaded when I noted I was only on page five of a staggering nineteen pages. She described a scenario of such intricate detail it would have had Tolkien throwing away his first manuscript of Lord of the Rings as 'too lightweight'. Her imaginative scene, complete with a detailed script, had a tragic grander of truly epic proportions. Homers Odyssey was a mere pamphlet in comparison. Sadly I'll never know how the tortuous storyline ended as boredom took over and I realised I could never afford the costumes or hire the required Nubian slave army.

I said, "Thanks but no thanks."

Number two started off with, "As a larger woman…" Which is as far as I got.

I said, "Thanks but no thanks."

Number three was fucking 'Diaper boy' yet again.

I said, "Bugger off."

Number four had a photo attached which I opened before reading the letter. Inexplicably it featured the correspondent inserting a carrot into a bodily orifice that was a fair distance from her mouth. Totally mystified by how this related to my post, it went straight into the bin.

Number five also featured an attached photo, which, very warily, I opened. I was confronted by a picture of a naked woman of almost skeletal proportions. I've honestly seen more meat on a butcher's apron. I say 'woman' but that's really just pure speculation as the aforementioned individual had so many piercings scattered around her body it was almost impossible to ascertain gender. Her letter commenced with 'I'm attracted to older men'. I think she really meant magnets. I concluded if I played with her I'd spend most of my time worrying about lightening strikes.

I said, "Thanks but no thanks."

Recognising that I was nearly half way through I felt the first hint of discouragement. I clicked on the next reply.

Number six started off swimmingly, a short intelligent note from someone who clearly understood this stuff. We were of like minds right up to the part where she said, "...so if you'd like to come to Vancouver."

I said, "Thanks but no thanks."

Number seven informed me that she was a 'figging' enthusiast which had me totally mystified (I'd been out of the scene for eight years). A quick check online revealed this was the eye watering practice of sticking a root of ginger up one's back passage. Now I've got no inherent problems with the 'tradesman's entrance' but combining it with a stem vegetable was unappealing. I briefly considered introducing her to correspondent number four before I said, "Thanks but no thanks."

Number eight unkindly informed me that I was a 'misogynist asshole who was going to burn in hell'. In fairness I suppose she was 50% accurate.

The next respondent described themselves as a 'passable transsexual' which made them sound like a dinner table condiment and the next was from Taiwan written in the most appalling English. She earnestly informed me she, 'Much enjoyed feelies'. I didn't know exactly what 'feelies' were but I had a fairly good idea and was pretty sure they had little to do with strict English discipline.

The remaining three however showed real promise. One was New Jersey based, which to my eternal credit I didn't hold against her and two were in Manhattan. I set about writing back. Clearly the playing field was as fecund as it had always been although my exposure to the mad people had previously been limited to reading Stacy's mail over three decades previously.

I comforted myself that evening by stripping Chloe to her white ankle socks in a candle lit room. Then, with 'Enigma's' soothing tones reverberating through the apartment, I subjected her to a prolonged beating with an authentic antique Lochgelley tawse, after which we shared a bottle of wine. All very civilised.

Some weeks and numerous emails and telephone conversations later, appointments had been arranged for all three. The women in question were all late thirties and gave good accounts of themselves. From what they said they'd had experience albeit nothing close to Chloe but understood what they were getting into. The first was due at 3pm on the Monday. The phone went at 2.30. "I'm awfully sorry," said woman number one, "The elevator has broken down in my apartment building so you'll understand that I'm a bit marooned till it gets fixed." I understood totally. Walking downstairs in a high rise is one thing, schlepping back up is quite another. "No problem," I murmured comfortingly, "What floor are you on by the way?"

There was a moment's hesitation, "The third," she confessed. Warning bells sounded like an imminent air raid. I wrote the next day cancelling. No kink is better than bad kink or, even worse, fat kink.

That evening I unwillingly attended a dinner with two clients and their wives. With a heavy heart I made my way to Soho dreading the evening ahead. I was correct in my predictions for the evening. Though the wine was modest, even in its limited quantities tongues became cringingly loosened towards the end of the evening. To my chagrin, erotic pursuits were brought into the conversation. Of course I love the subject but I prefer it to not to be discussed by semi inebriated simpletons to whom coloured condoms are considered a walk on the wild side. As the dialogue developed I didn't just bite my tongue, I almost chewed it off. Nonetheless I was a perfect gentleman.

I conducted myself with a self-effacement that bordered on martyrdom. I sat aghast as opinions and views were aired that were frankly best left unobserved…certainly by them. It really makes one wonder, if matters of the flesh are such a natural phenomenon, how come there are so many books about how to do it? I was informed slyly it was well known that while most people have sex lives, the English have hot-water bottles. Though there's a spirit of truth in this it was an observation that I received with an entertaining smile and a seething indignation. I continued masticating the remnants of what had once been my tongue and sank into the brandy whilst considering the arrival of number two on my list the following day. I wondered what my dinner companions would have made of it.

Woman number two walked over my threshold and introduced herself in a haze of frankly questionable perfume and a gushingly over familiarity which had my toes curling so much I felt I was wearing Arabian slippers. Her choice of attire was frankly challenging and the jeans size she'd selected to try and squeeze into was an ambitious choice.

Whilst her dress sense was certainly courageous, physically it has to be said she was also something of a challenge. On the plus side she sported a chest that caused me to duck whenever she turned suddenly, alas the same can also be said of her nose, a most unattractive appendage giving her a hawk like appearance reminiscent of an American Eagle. Whilst definitely no oil painting myself I only make these less than chivalrous observations as she was rather less than complimentary about me. Looking me up and down like a piece of meat she observed I, 'Really didn't make the best of myself'. God knows what had happened to the polite woman I'd spoken to on the telephone previously. I put it down to nerves. Remembering the specifics of her scene preferences (a misbehaving niece being dealt with by her uncle) I took her left earlobe between my thumb and forefinger and led her to the bedroom muttering, "You've asked for this young lady." Actually, she had, and I was annoyed.

Upon reaching the bedroom she said, "Would you like to see a photo of my previous disciplinarian?" "Now?" I said with some surprise. The photo was already in her hand. An enormous bear of a man welding a paddle confronted me. Not quite sure how to respond I was formulating a suitably neutral reply when I felt a hand grab me between the legs and heard her giggle, "Uncle always gave me a good fucking after he spanked me." An enduring image for some perhaps but not one that interested me at all. Looking at the guy it must have been like having a heavy clothes locker fall on you with the key still in the door. Talking of doors I showed her mine on the spot. She vanished quicker than dignity at a Sci Fi convention.

I was down to the last one. Hanna. Hanna had impressed me on the telephone. She appeared to be the sort of person who could hear the William Tell Overture and not think of The Lone Ranger. She was a lawyer. A lawyer who lived in a Park Avenue address so exclusive people actually got out of the bath to use the toilet. A lawyer who, in her own words, was looking to explore her limits. Yummy!

Chapter Eight

Paying to Play

Bloodied but unbowed by my recent experience it gave me a moment of pause. I realised for a day or so afterwards I hadn't been bouncing around in my normal effervescent fashion, fixing all and sundry with a rakish eye and exuding a genial bonhomie. Then I realised I never really did bounce around in an effervescent fashion, fixing all and sundry with a rakish eye and exuding a genial bonhomie, so I pressed on with my efforts.

True I'd not been entirely successful so far at re establishing a kink existence; though it was now definitely an aspect of my life again. Being the eternal optimist I considered myself to be on the right path yet something was missing. I knew what it was of course but I just didn't want to admit it to myself. I tried to ignore it to no avail. The genie was out of the bottle. I would go to sleep at night with the thoughts of it gently lapping at my brain like the waves on a distant tropical beach. Facing up to it would wreak havoc in my vanilla life…and yet…there it was… ever-present… quietly and persistently standing tiptoe in the wings of my psyche urging me on. The need to 'bottom'.

A problem indeed. When it came to kink it appeared I couldn't get a little bit pregnant. It was also a problem because, excuse the expression, I'm a very fussy bottom. If I'm being topped I'm always just moments away from flouncing out of the room like a petulant child if things aren't absolutely right. Back in the day I eventually whittled it down to only two people from our exclusive group who I could legitimately fess up to. One was my ex significant other and the other was Julia, a fearsome import from Germany. She could get me on my knees with the flick of an eyelid and inside my head in the time it took for her to say, "Prepare yourself."She 'had it'. With a great top I didn't need to worry about things being 'right', the quality of their dominance drove the scene and I'd be too busy trying to comply with her instructions and demands to even think about anything else.

Julia would beat her husband savagely and with great relish on a fairly regular basis. I was never even that convinced the poor sod was kinky. I just don't think he had any say in the matter. It was Julie's way or the highway. She arrived at one of our gatherings like a force of nature, statuesque yet svelte and resplendent in pencil skirt and tight white blouse. In her speech she was understated but her physical presence did all the talking. Studied, precise and cruel, she loved what she did and I loved her doing it. Once, whilst she was flogging my ex, she had her so apparently distressed I was about to step in and stop matters which was an absolute first. Julie laughed and purred, "She's loving it, aren't you my Liebling?" The quivering recipient offered a strangled, "Yes Mistress," between sobs. A great top indeed, she'd read her perfectly. She then subsequently led me to a quiet room away from the action and, with a cold thunder, beat me with a rubber strap for interrupting her. The marks lasted for six weeks. What? You want more details? Patience…it's coming…lots of it.

So, how to find a 'German Julia' in New York? I had no interest in going to fetish clubs or public parties so I consulted the oracle. Chloe was as ever full of sound advice. She was also recovering from her visit to 'Cardboard Box Man' who had an 'inventory fetish'. And you think I'm weird! Upon arrival at his apartment in the dark canyons of Roosevelt Island, she'd been logged in, assessed, bar coded, measured, stamped, appraised, and neatly packed into a large UPS box. Her shipping number was then solemnly logged into his meticulous computerised inventory system. And that was it. I think even Freud would have been stumped by that one. I guess it also says a fair bit about what it's like to live on Roosevelt Island.

She regaled me with a number of websites similar to the spanking page she'd steered me to initially. There were no women tops as far as I could see on the spanking site but she assured me that these more general BDSM sites did feature women who may fit the bill. What I found out was they mainly featured a very large number of desperately uninteresting people I had no wish to meet under any circumstances whatsoever. The vast majority seemed to be the sort of individuals who occasionally gazed out of their windows thinking, 'Yes, one day I will actually go outside'. A wretched hour on the net one evening convinced me I didn't have the time to waste to try and sort the wheat from the chaff, assuming of course there was any wheat to be found. I made a decision. A momentous decision and one I thought I'd never make. I'd try 'pay to play'. Not an ideal solution but surely it would make things easier? After all I knew a fair bit about professional Dominatrices.

What I found out was that I did indeed know a fair bit about Professional Dominatrices, but about professional Dominatrices some three decades plus previously. Back then Stacy's activities mainly consisted of hurting people and occasionally letting them worship her feet. A notable exception was 'Cupboard Boy', whose sole requirement was to be pushed into a wardrobe, have some handcuffs slapped on and a bucket of cold water thrown over him. A man of simple pleasures indeed and very much in the minority. In the main she beat, thrashed, whipped and tortured and occasionally tied people up for that purpose.

Things had changed. They'd changed an awful lot. I googled 'Dominatrix New York' and a gazillion Dominatrices sites popped up. I clicked on the first one. A pouting kitten in rubber appeared. Her site said she flogged, caned, spanked, whipped etc but what the bloody hell was 'T and D'? And 'Sissy Training'? I got the gist of what that was but how was this the work of a Pro Domme? 'Tickling'…err what? 'Forced Bi'? And 'orgasm control'? What was this 'chastity device' she spoke of? And what was abandonment play? And what for that matter what was 'Edge play?' And I didn't like the sound of 'financial domination' at all. 'NT'? What was an 'NT'? And 'Strap on play'? Dear God! Kink may be a broad church but I'm not religious but, mercifully I'm tolerant and relatively non judgemental about most things (unless we include the French). I concluded this domme was merely keeping all her options open, though, frankly, I didn't understand all the options and I wouldn't for some time.

After some exceedingly dull research it appeared virtually all her competitors were keeping all their options open as well until I came to realise the market had changed and I was way behind the times. From what I could ascertain discipline purists now seemed to be a very small sector of the economy.

Activities around medical play and needles were cringingly well represented. Bondage was clearly big business. Foot fetishists were apparently everywhere and Manhattan was demonstrably home to a plethora of men who wanted their orgasms controlled. My views on orgasm control (such as they are) are similar to my views on gun control. If there's one around, I want to control it.

I noted too that 'electrical play' (an oxymoron surely?) was now de rigueur with many of the sites featuring dommes proudly displaying their highly complex machines which were now manufactured specifically for the task of zapping ones undercarriage. I grimly recalled that this was one area of activity where I'd been an unwilling trailblazing pioneer.

Back in the day, whilst reluctantly indulging in the nightmare that is home decorating, I'd managed to fall from a ladder and injure my back. Much physiotherapy followed but I was dogged by continuing pain. At my wits end at the doctors one day he suggested that I might like to try a new experimental device. A pain management system based on sending an electrical current via adhesive pads to the affected area. My perverse partner had immediately thought of other possibilities but not of the possible consequences. I can't fault her creativity but I do vehemently critique her research and preparation.

One Sunday afternoon as I lay naked, bound, gagged and blindfolded, to my great alarm I felt her nimble fingers encapsulate my nether regions and attach the adhesive pads. She'd never used this machine before. I knew it to be capable of a fearsome jolt if the current regulators weren't turned down to zero before it was switched on. I tried to make this point but a gag is a gag so she mistook my muffled shrieks as normal play activity. A second or so later I was figuratively hanging from the ceiling by my fingernails with my hair on end whilst my almost ruined wedding tackle smoked alarmingly. Our relationship survived the experience but I never wore a gag again.

So, how to pick a dominatrix? A quandary indeed. I knew from my exposure to Stacy and her colleagues that pro dommes had only two things in common. Firstly they were women and secondly, they were kinky, or had been at some time in the past before they'd become totally jaded. Apart from that, unsurprisingly, they were all different. This hard gleaned 'inside information' helped me not one bit in my selection process.

I didn't want anyone too young. They wouldn't have the skill sets or indeed the maturity to top someone approaching his late thirties. Oh alright then, his late forties. Whilst they didn't need to have the body of a catwalk model they needed to be in a semblance of shape. Additionally they needed to share my interests i.e. discipline and have a measure of intelligence. Stunning beauty, whilst not a pre requisite, would certainly not be frowned upon.

Some of these criteria I thought I could ascertain by the websites though I suspected Photoshop had been working overtime on some of the images. Intelligence could perhaps be judged by the thoughtfulness of the verbiage. And as for interests, well most of them seemed to list what they did so that should help. Well, it didn't.

Two weary hours later, with eyes resembling fried eggs, I pulled myself away from the computer totally 'pro dommed' out. I'd probably gone though around thirty sites from the hundreds available. So far, in terms of 'interests', pretty much everyone seemed to do everything (whatever 'everything' actually was). Additionally they all looked great. I took a deep breath, picked one of the thirty at random, and wrote a short polite note to the woman concerned. I recalled that timewasters were an endemic problem in a pro dommes life so I endeavoured to ooze sincerity.

Surprisingly a reply arrived back within ten minutes. I guessed it was a slow day. It said, 'Tk U 4 Yr note. When do u want to cum see me?'

I considered the question for a moment and concluded that 'Never' was the answer. An answer which I had the courtesy of actually sending back in the Queens English.

I tried number two on the list. Mistress Lyra looked like she had what it took so I clicked on the send button and crossed my fingers. An email exchange ensued which resulted in me standing on a pre arranged street corner downtown whilst I called her for the final address. It felt most incongruous. An early Friday evening in New York. Throughout the city the young, rich and beautiful would be primping themselves up for an exciting Manhattan evening. Fine fragrances were being sprayed onto intimate body parts. Lithe young feminine bodies were being eased into skin-tight jeans and eager conversations no doubt abounded as to the preferred destination for the evening's entertainment. And there was I skulking around nefariously on a street corner waiting to be beaten! A class act indeed. I couldn't help but think of how appalled my dear departed mother would have been. I made the call to my chastiser only to have her say (and this is absolutely true!), "Can you call back in ten minutes? I'm having trouble getting my boots on." With a heavy heart I did so and followed her directions to the appointed location.

I rang the bell and the entrance opened, my prospective tormenter skulking unseen behind the door away from prying eyes. I walked in and realised that there had been a case of mistaken identity. This wasn't 'Mistress Lyra' at all, it was 'Goddess Grossly Overweight' together with her evil smelling mongrel dog who promptly and with great enthusiasm buried his nose in my crotch. As a common courtesy I paid her tribute fee and was back out on the street in a heartbeat. The entire encounter had lasted less than a minute. My itch remained resolutely unscratched and my wallet was a tad lighter.

As I stood on a street corner in bemused amazement my cell trilled. I grouchily answered it to hear 'Gay Marks' effete voice inviting me out for the evening. Outrageous though he may have been, he was never boring and I thought he'd lift my flagging spirits. The early evening saw me quaffing beer while he held court. Halfway through him detailing the recent depravities he'd been involved in I said, "I've known you long enough Mark, you can't shock me." "Oh no?" he said, "You have no idea." I did of course, I'd seen him coming out of Leatherman. Tiresomely he insisted that we move onto one of his gay clubs as he said 'something special' was going on that evening. I could hardly wait...

Mark delighted in taking me out of my comfort zone and gay clubs always did that. By now though I was getting used to it. We walked into his preferred destination. 'Something special' was BDSM night and it was full of Leatherman customers or at least that what I assumed by looking at the clubbers. Arseless chaps and moustaches abounded. Impossibly fit men with glistening muscles strode around flexing their sinews in an orgy of leather and lubricant. I knew a lot about BDSM but I didn't know anything about gay BDSM. The first thing I did learn was that these guys play hard, really hard.

I watched horrified as one poor sod took a paddle stroke so intense it actually broke across his butt whilst at the same time literally lifting the recipient of his feet. This was serious stuff. Mark grinned at me in the knowledge that I was so far out of the comfort box I couldn't even see where I'd left the box. Or so he thought. I edged my way around a lithe naked young man who'd been strung up in order that passers by could adorn him with clothespins. He had so many attached he looked more hedgehog than human.

We grabbed a drink at the bar and retired to a quieter corner of the establishment with some of his friends. As we talked I noticed an archetypal gay figure complete with the officers cap and cross-banded leather chest piece string up a semi naked guy who I assumed was his slave. As he did so Mark said, "Hey look, Paul's going to do his stuff." With that the aforesaid Paul produced a single tail and went to work on his supplicant with probably the worst technique I've ever seen. He was clueless. My host nudged me and grinned. "Well you can't say I've not managed to shock you this time." "You have," I agreed, "His technique is total crap." We fixed eyes for a moment.

Without saying a word he got up and approached the whipper. They talked for a few moments then both came back to the table. "You can do better?" Paul asked, with, in fairness to him, only a modicum of sarcasm. "Actions speak louder than words," I replied and held my hand out for the implement. Marks face was a picture. Paul smirked, "You're kidding me?" I took the whip and remarked unsmilingly, "I never kid about single tail."

I walked up to the supplicant. A big guy, he was in great shape, around six two and probably two hundred pounds. "Can you take this stuff?" I enquired, "I mean really take it?" "It's my fourth time," he replied. "That's not what I asked slave," I replied evenly, "I said can you take it?" His look gave him away. I saw the hint of nervousness in his eyes as he saw the commitment in mine. "If you say stop, I'll stop and I won't start again. It'll be over. Do you understand?" He nodded. I grabbed his hair and pulled his head back sharply. "Very well," I murmured, "Don't disappoint me."

By now Mark, Paul et al were out of their seats. I walked back and told them to keep a safe distance away. As I did so a few other people strolled over to see what was going on. "Guys," I said, "This is a four foot single tail and I'm going to be moving around so I need at a circle width of at least ten to twelve feet for safety or someone's going to loose an eye." They moved back as yet more curiosity seekers arrived.

I looked at the whip. A cheap example not yet broken in. A newbie's implement. I swung it languidly from side to side then, with a flourish, I swung it above my head, executed two full overhead circles completing the second with a deafening crack. Pure theatre. I was now very much the object of attention. I swung the whip backwards and forward, measuring the distance between me and the slave and planted my feet when the light flicks just touched his back. This would be my ground zero, my 'working point'.

I started with light over arm flicks just touching his back with the lightest of kisses from the tip of the whip. I worked across and then down and then randomly so he never knew which area I was going to hit next. I continued, slowly building the intensity until the slave was twitchy with the discomfort. Planting my right foot firmly I put my left foot way behind me thus moving my torso more than four foot from the recipient. At that moment I let loose with an airburst. This involves cracking the whip just inches above the slaves skin so powerfully that they can feel the wind. The noise is dramatic and totally messes with the recipient's sensibilities. I caught Marks slack jawed face in the crowd.

Moving my left foot back to ground zero I started weaving the whip in a figure of eight, increasing the speed slowly. I inched forward so that each cross swing caught the slave across the top of his back in rapid succession. By now he was sweating and beginning to writhe. I paused momentarily for effect, I raised my right hand and with my left I lifted the tip of the whip over my head and behind my neck. I then released the tip so's it hung over my left shoulder. With a rapid twist of my right hand I pulled the whip round the back of my neck, swinging backhand from left to right. The tip caught the slave in the left middle of his back leaving a livid line. I got my first cry of pain.

Cries of pain are easy to get in single tail sessions. Unless your sub is a full-blown hard-core masochist (and I mean really full blown) you can 'safe word' them very swiftly by going too hard to quickly. Single tails, for me, are elegant and sophisticated and therefore so should a session be. That's how I like to play. It's a dance, bringing someone close to safe wording then easing back and then, just when they've relaxed a little, coming back with a vengeance pushing them further.

A few more similar throws later I switched to side-to-side slashes generated purely from the wrist working his sides from waist to shoulder. I increased the intensity then pulled back now executing lighter overhead strokes but using more than just the tip of the whip. The lines on his back were now starting to build up in earnest and made for a spectacular visual sight. The audience was totally silent. I then planted my left foot and stepped forward with my right putting me closer to the slave. I then executed more side-to-side slashes, the difference being this time I was nearer so they wrapped around to the front of his body. I started to get some shrieks.

The slave was clearly in a different world, not knowing how much each stroke was going to hurt and not knowing where the next throw was going to land or what sort of stroke it would be. I stepped back to ground zero and gave him the lightest flick in the middle of his back then followed it up with a thundering 'Napalm stroke'. That's a full-blown stroke of the whip using all its length. The slave shouted out as a deep red welt developed in a dramatic line leading all the way from his right shoulder to the left hand side of his waist. I stopped for a moment and threw another napalm, this time from left to right. The slave literally shouted blue murder.

I paused again then delivered three two more criss cross napalms back to back. The slave screamed, "Enough enough enough." I was impressed. He'd done well. I furled the whip and with a sly grin took a bow and was stunned to receive a round of applause. Mark approached, "I'm fucking speechless," he stumbled. So at least I achieved something valuable that evening.

A week or so later saw me bent over a stool in a neat little apartment somewhere in midtown. An effete Siamese cat gazed at me languorously from her vantage point on a nearby sofa. I think I sensed vague disapproval in her eyes but I wasn't sure. I was too busy enduring the relentless ear bashing that I was being subjected to by the women I'd paid to beat me. The lady concerned was both attractive and petite. She'd replied to my introductory note, asked a few pertinent questions then written to me saying she, 'Knew exactly what I wanted and I was to say no more as she would create a scene especially for me.' Whilst it would be imprudent to suggest psychic dommes don't exist, I felt fairly confident she wasn't one. I told her I appreciated her pro-active approach but I really didn't think I'd even begun to tell her enough but she'd hear no more of it. I decided to give her the benefit of the doubt. Was this perhaps true actual dominance I was hearing?

At that moment I'd been in her apartment for almost forty minutes, for most of which time I'd been subject to a protracted haranguing that was about as convincing as power sharing talks on the Korean peninsula. Eventually I could take no more. Standing up I remarked (with due respect) I was not paying her to talk, well not talk that much anyway and could she kindly bloody well get on with it. The moment I said those words I knew it was over. The moment hadn't just passed, it'd vanished as if it had never existed. Yet another tribute paid with nothing happening.

Two further disasters later I was on the verge of giving up. One involved a domme who was jumpier than a box of frogs with the confidence of a lion tamer deprived of their chair and the second? Well, lets just not even go there eh? When you don't even know the correct names for your own implements it's a warning shot across the bows. Additionally, this womans deportment suggested she couldn't knock the skin off a rice pudding, let alone anything else. Four visits and four tributes paid and not yet a single stroke delivered. This pay for play business was getting expensive. Where were the German Julias and Stacys of this world?

Despite some of my less than charitable observations regarding the pro dommes I initially met, my respect for how they tried to earn a living remained (and remains) undiminished. They have to invest in all manner of sometimes very expensive equipment and clothing in the hope that they'll get a return on it. They have to put up with all sorts of crap from time wasters, no hopers, would be romantics and rampaging perverts, some with tastes that would shake the most sturdy countenance. No shows, bad hygiene (and of course bad spelling), unrealistic requests, fawning, stalking, unwanted attention, last minute cancellations, whining, obsessives, wankers, sundry dickheads and of course people like me…and that's just a shortened list. The few women that make a truly good living out of this business long term, and there are really very few, have seriously worked at it. They possess the patience of Job and the pragmatism of Solomon. They deal with on a daily basis that which would drive the average person to despair. No, they're not all angels but they're all human beings. It's not 'easy money' and never ever be persuaded it is. They work bloody hard for it.

Deconstructing the various experiences I'd had to date I realised that most of these women, quite understandably, were trying to make money out of this business by offering the widest possible range of services to attract as many people as they could. They were generalists. Specialisation was clearly a more risky proposition and from a business point of view I totally understood that. That being said, my greater understanding of dominatrices business models wasn't getting me any closer to my objective. I decided to have one last try. I'm glad I did. If I hadn't I'd have never met 'Domme Jackeline'.

Her website was noticeable insomuch as the lists of her 'don'ts' were almost as long as her list of 'do's'. And her list of 'do's' was one of the shortest I'd seen. There was focus…I approved. The verbiage was supremely confident without being strident and clearly written by someone who had thought about dominance real or pretended and how to best portray it in an unambiguous yet tempting way. She had declined to show her face in the photos. Visually they showed very little save for the fact that she was in shape and sported a most fetching brunette bob whilst leaving imagination to do most of the work. I made an appointment.

By now I felt like a combat hardened veteran of such encounters. I knew the drill. You turn up at a strange woman's abode, give her some money and then promptly leave. Hmm maybe this was what 'financial domination' was. I'd now entered my experiences into my long list of life's hard learned lessons. Number twenty-seven, 'Never visit a professional dominatrix for the first time with your hopes up'. It was right there under number twenty-six which said, 'Never, ever, be persuaded to go and see a movie which features a woman on the poster wearing no make up'. Guys, you know it's true.

At the appointed hour I stood in front of my proscribed tormentor. With an instantly dry throat I handed over the fee in the knowledge that this time it wouldn't be wasted money. I was as mesmerised as a hungry newborn baby in a topless bar. This woman 'had it'. In fact she more than 'had it', she defined it. She was it's personification. Sometimes you just know. Around six foot in heels, she was adorned in a tight black armless one piece dress which reached half way down her stocking clad thighs. Her sleek countenance was a study in understatement. Picking my jaw up off the floor I followed her meekly through her immaculate apartment into the room where she evidently conducted her business. Eight long bottoming free years were about to come to an end. A part of me wished she wasn't 'right'. That way I could still legitimately leave, head held high, knowing I had kept up my elite standards whilst as the same time not actually having to endure the pain and indignity of being beaten. At that point I didn't need to indulge in any fruitless speculation inquiring for whom the bell was tolling. I knew this time it was tolling for me and the sound was deafening.

She pleasantly bade me sit on a chair whilst she made herself comfortable opposite and started asking questions. Questions that indicated both a razor sharp intelligence and a total grasp of the subject in hand. Her voice indicated European origins with a precise diction and an economy of words. An economy of words was an apt description for me too at that moment. Almost speechless, I was nervous as a long tailed cat in a room full of rocking chairs. Her calm demeanour and deliberate mannerisms were demonstrations of a true top at work. Assured control. And yes, thankfully, she was very easy on the eye.

When I was able to string more than two words together without stammering I was deliberately circumspect regarding her enquiries about my own kink background. No one likes a smart arse and, as it had been so long since I'd played I felt was I almost a newbie again. I indicated that I'd had some experience but deliberately offered few details. She asked what my preferred fantasies were but try as I might I couldn't seem to focus on the question. My blood was pumping and my adrenalin rate was sky high. Half way through my incoherent waffling she said, just sharply enough to make me jump, "Shhhh. I want you to strip and stand with your nose against the wall and wait until I return." And with that she left the room.

Two minutes later I was naked, standing as I had been instructed whilst trying to process what had happened. I'd complied with her request, no, I'd complied with her *instruction*, without hesitation and yet I hadn't t even told her what I really liked. Why didn't I say something? Wasn't I dominant? Wasn't I the paying customer? An experienced top with many years before the mast? How could she play with me without knowing what I liked? It was almost as if in the previous fifteen minutes a stranger had entered my body. She walked back into the room and, covering my modesty, I half turned and opened my mouth to speak. She grabbed my head and firmly returned my nose to the wall. "I never said you could speak," she said calmly. I felt my knees weaken. Not only did she 'have me', I knew I was no longer in control. Power had been exchanged.

This element is so often misunderstood by so many. Real power is never given up, it's taken! I had given nothing to Domme Jackeline. She had grabbed my power the moment she set eyes on me. I should have seen it coming. I do it all the time. It's a real and palpable thing. She was so good she'd done it before I even had the chance to notice what was happening. A true master (or mistress) of her art. The real article. As these thoughts rushed through my head I realised that she hadn't even hit me yet. Out of the corner of my eye I saw her raise her hand to flick back a misplaced hair. I saw muscle definition in her arm. Jesus!

"Over my knee," she snapped. I turned to see her primly sitting in a chair motioning to the appropriate place. Feeling like a total idiot at the incongruity of the situation I once again gave thanks for the absence of my mother and acquiesced to her demand. As I bent over I felt the blood rush to my head and the hint of a cool breeze on my derriere from a slightly open window. "Very well," she said, "Lets see what you're made of," and with that she made 'first contact'. My long wait was over.

It was more of a shock than anything else. A sharp sting, only a few stages up from a baby slap (not that I've ever slapped a baby but I've certainly felt like it). It was tolerable and embarrassing. I cursed myself. I felt so bloody stupid. Why the hell did I want to do this? And for that matter it was costing me hard cash. Her cadence increased as did the intensity, her strikes covering every part of my rear. Suddenly she stopped. "Hmm," she murmured, "I can see you've played quite heavily before." Sometimes when spanking you can see the ghosts of old marks stimulated by the increased blood flow. I made to acquiesce. "Silence," she snapped and started spanking again in earnest.

Some ten minutes in I was definitely uncomfortable. Mr Super Experienced Hard Core himself was having trouble with a hand spanking. I couldn't believe how hard this woman could whale. She stopped briefly and I exhaled sharply. No sooner had I done so then she started again, this time with a fearsome hairbrush and, boy did she lay it on. I started squirming. "Be still," she ordered. I gritted my teeth and endeavoured to comply. This was absolutely no fun at all. She started again even harder. Just as we got to the stage where I was about to shout out, "Fuck me that's enough already!" she stopped. "On your feet," she ordered. I leapt up and rubbed my butt furiously. I'd seriously forgotten how much this stuff hurt. "I didn't say you could rub," she admonished. With that she pulled me back over her lap and began again with the hairbrush...dear God!

This is the dichotomy that some of us kinksters face when we bottom. A lot of us aren't masochists. We don't love the pain, we love the thought of the activity and the long delicious lead up. We enjoy the feelings afterwards and the come down and the replaying of it in our minds over and over again. But of course to get to enjoy all that we've got to physically go through the actual discipline. It's a necessary evil. I was being sharply reminded of that right now.

"Up," she commanded, "And bend over the chair with your hands on the seat." I followed her order with an understandable alacrity and I most certainly didn't rub my butt although I desperately wanted to do so. As my heartbeat settled down slightly I felt something tap gently on my right buttock cheek. A nano second later I felt the blaze as she brought down a leather strap across both off them. I leapt up clutching the target area. In shock I turned angrily around, "Jesus fucking

Christ," I snapped, "That really fucking hurt!" We fixed gazes. She looked straight back at me expressionless, totally unfazed. I relaxed slightly with a hint of a smile and offered, "I guess on a list of stupid things to say to a dominatrix that's pretty close to the top." We both exploded into laugher. A truly wonderful moment.

In the past that sort of moment would have been a scene ender but not for Domme Jackeline it wasn't. Once the laughter was over she was all business again. "Back into position," she ordered, "Head down," and she continued for a further twenty-three agonising strokes. I was seriously considering flipping open my communicator and shouting, "Beam me up Scotty, right now for Chrissakes. "No time for that however as I was being ordered to lie on the bed. For my moments hesitation she gave me another six full force strokes. When she finished I practically ran to the bed, any attempt at retaining even a modicum of dignity was long gone. I was just holding on by my fingernails trying to get through this. I knew already that I was never going to do this again…yeah right!

I lay on the bed tenser than, well, something that's very tense indeed. My arse was on fire. Jackeline soothed, "Breath deeply," and unloaded a further eighteen strokes with a vicious black tawse. With that she left the room, returning a minute or so later with a bowl of ice cubes. "My, but you're a marker," she said and started running an ice cube over the affected area. "It helps with the bruising," she offered. "Well, I made it through didn't I?" I breathed with relief. She laughed a laugh that I was going to get to know very well. "Don't be silly," she said, "I've still got to cane you yet." I turned around in genuine alarm and caught her eye. "Don't speak," she said. In that moment I knew I'd take the strokes, in fact I knew I'd take any amount of strokes she had to offer. I felt a warmth envelop me and goose pimples on my flesh. I allowed myself to indulge in the very temporary luxury of believing the fantasy. I wanted to take the strokes. To take them for her. Not only was she a true top she was also a true professional. She'd totally got my mark and was going to ruthlessly exploit it accordingly. I recognised this and completely respected it. Fair 'do's'. Business is business. Quality demands respect and she had mine. The enveloping warmth wasn't of much use when she got the cane out. "What's the most you've ever had with one of these?" she asked as she swished it ominously though the air. I thought for a moment and lied smoothly, "Err around sixty." "Then you shall have seventy," she replied. And that's what I had. I thought I was going to die.

I didn't die but I nearly did once I returned home and examined the damage. Though I'm the first to admit that one cannot make an omelette without breaking eggs, I was chagrined to realise that I'd certainly be out of the dating scene for the next couple of weeks. The area was beyond crimson, it was a blazing scarlet replete with perfectly placed purple tramlines from the cane. This woman had the skill sets aright. Even though I'd been in her company for a mere ninety minutes and paid through the nose for the privilege I was sure of one thing. I'd met my kink nemesis.

Chapter Nine

An Embarrassment of Riches

Hanna thought it would be a good idea to meet at a quality rendezvous and get to know each other before we actually did anything. Thinking it an eminently sensible idea I concurred, knowing from our telephone exchanges, if nothing else, she'd be intelligent company. Discrete oblique questioning had revealed she wasn't of an 'ample countenance' and she'd offered her age without prompting. She suggested an exclusive venue just off Fifth Avenue a few blocks south of Central Park and I suppressed the gut wrenching feeling I always get when being asked to part with large sums of money. Well, actually, on being asked to part with any sums of money really. The last time I dined at this location I'd made the mistake of calling the wine waiter over for a recommendation. He arrived at the table sporting an entertaining hairpiece of dubious extravagance and a supercilious demeanour, both of which failed to meet with my approval. The other thing which failed to meet with my approval were his wine selections as, much to my chagrin,

I'd failed to win the lottery yet again that week. I am reliably informed though that ones chances are significantly improved by actually buying a ticket. But, I digress...

Clearly a huge step up from the other Internet sourced subs I'd previously encountered (Chloe being a notable exception) I felt I owed Hanna the courtesy of a half decent presentation. I dressed in arrogantly fashionable Kenzo trousers, cutting edge Prada shoes and a languidly indulgent Georgio Armani shirt complimented by pernicious cologne the like of which only Bulgari can create. Giving myself a cheeky yet satisfactory grin in the mirror, I decided to further affect my sense of bohemian elan by not wearing a tie. It's the closest I ever get to 'going commando' but it's a statement nevertheless, albeit, I admit, a remarkably small one.

Arriving at the establishment exuding an air of totally misplaced confidence I barked my name to the Maître 'D' with a studied brusqueness. He discreetly observed that my flies were not merely undone but actually gaping. Mortally humiliated I gratefully slipped him a twenty and was led to our table by a nauseatingly unctuous waiter to find Hanna already in situe. As I sat I tried to ignore the fact that she was staring at me as if she was purchasing a used car.

Hanna of course wasn't her real name. Her parents originally hailed from Denmark. I am embarrassed to report that even now, after having it irritably repeated to me on numerous occasions, the nuances of its pronunciation still elude me. I do know it requires making a sound similar to vomiting combined with full mouthful of salvia prior to producing a championship distance spit.

She was nervous and I endeavoured to be understanding. Rather than railroad our dialogue towards the reason for meeting I indulged her in her opening gambit of general conversation. We discussed business, global affairs, financial matters and the state of the weather. Anything other than kink. I acquiesced with a purported knowledge of geo politics that would have had the BBC's chief political correspondent choking on his food. I made sweeping statements on various economic matters that would have had a Wall Street analyst scratching his head in dismay. I offered insights as to the perniciousness of antidisestablishmentarianism and purred engagingly about the prospects for world peace. I seemed to have effectively made it past the first few intellectual hurdles before I cranked my act up a gear and attempted to gently steer matters to the reason for our meet.

She deflected the attempt and turned the conversation to art. She really was nervous. Concerning art it has been reliably reported that the word 'philistine' has often been used about me regarding such matters (quite legitimately). Nonetheless a lively discussion developed as to the pro and cons of various artists. Hanna demanded, "If you were in The Guggenheim and it caught fire and you only had time to save one piece which one would it be?" I thought on this for a moment and replied, "The one nearest the door."

She laughed and finally started to relax. I in turn relaxed as well and started to let her discover my good qualities without my help. Actually of course that's normally never a problem, in fact I've always been inordinately proud of my modesty and take great pains to constantly remind people of it.

Her nervousness was most understandable. Our encounter was like a cross between a job interview and a blind date. I once read that one of the few differences between a blind date and a job interview is with a job interview it's fairly unlikely that you're going to end up naked at the end of it. With a kink first encounter there's the same stress except with the added pressure of knowing you're not going to be just naked at the end of it, you're going to be consensually abused as well.

In her endeavours to secure herself a sound thrashing her experiences with men mirrored my own experiences with women since I'd been living in NYC. We laughed and shared stories of our nightmares. She very much reminded me of the people I'd played with back in the day. Intelligent, professional, in shape, non needy and enthusiastic. Of course they're out there but, inevitably, so are the frogs. Frogs? Well, we both concluded that to get kink as part of your life one needs to be prepared to do a lot of frog kissing. We'd also both got to the stage where we felt we'd puckered up to quite enough slimy amphibians.

Hanna had had the spanking bug as far back as she could remember. Upon her divorce some two years previously she'd decided to address this part of her personality. Despite her broad hints, her marriage had been woefully spank free and apart from a few playful slaps from old boyfriends she'd never experienced it. The instant her separation papers were signed she'd plunged headlong into Internet hell to scratch the itch, an itch that had yet to be scratched.

At her first encounter she'd smelled the heavy aroma of Ben Gay well before her would be potential chastiser had even entered the restaurant. By the time the trembling octogenarian had finally perambulated himself to her table the evening was practically gone as was Hanna's patience.

Number two was a man apparently disconnected to the point of autism. Almost an idiot savant with the emphasis on the word idiot. His dinner choices consisted of ordering two desserts...together. Hanna realized almost immediately that this was someone who spent way too much time memorising telephone directories and bus timetables; time he should have been spending attending to his personal hygiene. She'd hit the wine to try and make the encounter go more quickly but had discovered that sometimes too much drink just isn't enough!

Despite significantly tightening her selection processes the dross continued to find holes in her protective armour. Number three had obviously had extensive plastic surgery but sadly the visual evidence suggested that the procedures had been undertaken by a surgeon who'd probably qualified online. His visage made her feel that she'd erroneously stumbled into a reject from Madame Tussauds. A dress sense that reflected 'New Jersey Shore' chique didn't help matters either. Neither did the fact that the guy was a red head, which was obviously a deal breaker. Of course, though it's well documented (and I believe now scientifically proven) that ginger haired men were born without a soul, I'm also personally convinced that it's the Devils mark!

And so it went on. With me she'd just hit double figures. I was number ten. She was certainly persistent. I was impressed

I enquired as to how she had decided to respond to my post amongst the huge number of terminally sad men on the site (naturally excluding myself from that description). Her reply was unexpected and leads me now to unashamedly paraphrase the first lines of 'War of the Worlds'. I would have never believed that my 'affairs were being watched from afar'. My exceedingly modest online activity had come to the attention of the woman I was to eventually christen 'Pernicious Penny'.

Penny was a woman in Boston with whom Hanna had formed an online friendship in recent weeks. It appears that Penny had long since passed the frog kissing stage and was keenly focussed on quality play. Hawk like she'd noticed my original posting and the subsequent changing of the wording to include 'Englishman'. After that change she'd pounced and immediately suggested Hanna 'give me a go' and report back her findings. Though she hadn't met me she reportedly felt the way my post read, together with the fact I was a Brit, warranted further investigation. Apparently she monitored the 'spanking radar' with the precision of an air traffic controller. I silently thanked both Chloe for her posting advice and this mysterious Penny for helping set up a meet that apparently wasn't wasting my time either. I resolved to learn more about this woman.

Back at my apartment Hanna explained her fantasies. She was, by her own admission, on occasion, the 'Troll bitch from Hell' at the office. When things were going badly she'd treat her staff appallingly and scared everyone to death. Her scenario was simple. In her 'head' the senior partner of her Law firm had sent her to me to be punished for her attitude. In future he would repeat this for any further such transgressions. A nice simple scenario. I approved.

As it was her first time I did her the courtesy of reminding her this activity did actually hurt. She looked at me as if I was a blithering idiot. As a newbie I also gave her a two stage safe word. "Amber' meaning 'ease off a bit' and 'red' meaning stop. Essentially I was putting her in control for our initial confrontation. And so we began. It was amusing to see a hard-bitten Manhattan lawyer standing with her nose pressed to the wall with her hands on her head. I resisted making the obvious smart assed comments I so desperately wanted to make and lectured her sternly on the instructions I'd 'received' from her employer.

"I'm informed," I began, "Your behaviour at the office has been less than satisfactory, however the nature of your transgressions are of no interest to me whatsoever. I have been instructed that you are to be punished for these infractions and, as a professional disciplinarian, I have been tasked to give you a serious thrashing. Do you understand?" There was inevitably the hint of a giggle. I quickly walked over to her, pulled up her skirt and gave her resoundingly sound slap on the back of her right thigh. She turned around with a face like thunder. I put my finger over her lips as she was about to speak. I looked directly at her, "Leave now or stay and do as you're told. I won't repeat myself." She was momentarily frozen. The shock of the pain and my sudden attitude change piercing her comfort bubble. I had her.

"Remove your skirt immediately and quickly," I said calmly. I then had the wonderful experience of seeing this inordinately high priced attorney fumbling around like nervous schoolgirl trying to get the article off in the shortest possible time. A moment later she was over my lap. I unceremoniously pulled her panties down to her ankles "We certainly won't be needing these will we?" I inquired. There was no response. I gave her a firm slap on her left thigh and was rewarded with the hint of a squeak. "I said we won't be needing these will we? I repeated. "No sir," was the even toned reply.

"Very well," I continued, "Put your hands on the floor and spread your fingers. Put your head down and put the front of your feet on the floor." She complied. "Do you know why I want your feet like that?" I enquired. She shook her head. I planted another firm slap across the back of her thigh "I can't hear you," I admonished. "No Sir. I don't know why," she replied with slight shake in her voice. "Because it makes it more difficult to clench your cheeks, that's why," I responded, and with that I started with baby slaps to warm her up.

She was enduring stoically. I knew she'd be trying to process the thoughts running through her head. She'd be thinking, "I'm actually doing it at last." "I can deal with this level of pain'." "How much worse is it going to get?" "Is this like I thought it would be?" "I am/am not enjoying this," and inevitably, "Does he think my butt looks big?" It didn't. It was pert and delightful.

I upped the cadence and intensity but still no protestations were received from my lap. She was certainly enduring a fairly robust hand spanking with hardly a wiggle. I was impressed. For a first timer she was certainly sucking it up. With that I bade her stand up and totally remove her panties from round her ankles. A moment later she was lying over a chair with her hands on the floor. "Ten strokes with my belt," I informed her. I unleashed a medium stroke. Quite a shock for a newbie. It was evidently not a shock for Hanna. She barely moved. By strokes eight nine and ten there was certainly twitching but nothing like I expected. I took a medium strap to her. She was still silent on stroke four. I 'checked in' with her. "If you remember your safe word say 'yes sir'." "Yes sir," she replied breathlessly. Ten strokes of the strap later I'd still not heard a major sound.

"Right stand up," I said, "Put your legs two feet apart and rest your hands on your knees." She complied immediately, her face scarlet. I produced a paddle. A fairly modest example around eighteen inches long and a third of an inch thick. Though modest this sucker would sting. "Prepare for six," I instructed, "If your hands come off your knees we'll start again." With the first stroke I got a big exhale and her whole body twisted but she kept her hands on her knees. She repeated the same violent motion for each of the strokes. I was now very seriously impressed. I'd never met a newbie like this before. Indeed, if it wasn't for the state of her rear I'd have assumed she was lying about having no experience. Her bottom was now showing signs of wear and tear. I was curious to see how far I could take her but naturally I didn't want to do any serious damage.

Next I had her lying on the bed with a pillow under her middle to keep her butt raised. I checked in with her again but she was most definitely still compos mentis. I then delivered eighteen strokes with a medium level cane. Each stroke had her arching and twisting but still not a sound. Amazing. By this time her buttocks were a livid red and, for a first timer, she'd most certainly had enough both physically and mentally.

"Very well young lady," I advised, "I've finished." I then added in my normal jovial fashion, "Very well done Hanna, very well done indeed. You've finally had that thrashing you always dreamed of."

She looked up at me with a face that showed so many emotions. She tried to form a word then her face crumpled up and she burst into tears. I went to get some tissues and as I handed her one she suddenly burst out laughing. This continued for a minute until the tears came back Once again, a minute later she was laughing. I'd never seen anything like it. She finally managed to speak. "I can't describe what I'm feeling," she gasped, "That was fantastic, absolutely fantastic. I'm floating. I just want to explode." Then back came the tears followed once again by the laughing. Clearly she was in 'endorphin central'. A delicious place to be.

If you're kinkster you'll 'get' all of the above. If you're not you won't. It's as simple as that. Good kink can be almost spiritual sometimes. It can take you to places you didn't know were there. There is an enormous amount of literature on the subject where the learned (and the patently not so learned) opine about such matters. Various luminaries offer complex deconstructions on the minutiae of play, its motivations and results and its almost endless combinations and intellectual permutations. I'm not going to add to that as I've nothing additional to say and it's also not what this book is about. Suffice to say that Hanna left emotionally exhausted and happy, very happy indeed, but not before she'd given me 'Pernicious Penny's' email address.

Having made some good progress in my endeavours, the thought of sorting through more Internet rubbish was about as appealing as the prospect of reading *The Celestine Prophecy* a second time. Or for a first time for that matter. Despite the surprisingly constant trickle of new enquiries from my post, I instigated a draconian selection policy which would have made an ultra right wing eugenics fanatic blanche at my extremism. I decided my frog kissing days were well behind me. No oldies, fatties or newbies and I demanded proof. No weirdos, partner seekers, romantics or obsessives. Be intelligent (a mandatory requirement), funny if possible and sane. Subsequent to those criteria being in place only two more individuals ever made it through my entrenched defences from that source. 'Single tail Celeste' and 'Trust Fund Trudy.' about whom more later.

So, who was this apparently matriarchal Penny in Boston? Why did she keep such a close eye on the spanking radar? Hanna had spoken of her with some reverence and she wasn't easy to impress. Did such monitoring of Internet spanking minutia indicate obsessivness? And, really, hadn't I been spending way too much of my time on this nonsense recently anyway? I concluded I had. I now had two regular spankees, I'd single tailed some poor guy half to death and Domme Jackeline had help me scratch my bottoming itch. That was surely enough to keep me going. I did have things to do with my time other than deal with the disciplinary needs of recalcitrant women. Additionally, Domme Jackeline had ensured that with my butt in its distressed condition, I was currently depriving numerous waif thin teenage catwalk models the opportunity of sleeping with me. Yes enough was enough for the moment. I'd give it a rest. Boston could wait.

On the plane to the Massachusetts Capital that weekend I cursed my lack of resolve. I eventually consoled myself the film director Jim Cameron was maybe right in his assertion that sometimes 'More is more'. Surely after eight kink free years I was entitled? And Penny had sounded like great fun on the phone. Direct questioning had confirmed she fitted my eugenics template and anyway, I'd never been to Boston. At least it would allow me to incorrectly boast that I'd been to Harvard. Pointedly ignoring the attempt of the man next to me to engage me in conversation, I snuggled down to contemplate the approaching encounter. The guy had such a spectacular 'comb over' I was continually trying to stop giggling. What is it about these men? Do they think no one will notice? I guess when you honestly believe that Sudoku is a suitable topic of conversation, personal appearance is an irrelevance. Oh, and anyway, Penny had invited her friend Jeanine, a fellow spankee, to fly in from Chicago to join us for some fun. It had been a long time since I dealt with two naughty girls at once and it would have been downright rude to refuse. At least that's my excuse.

A short while later I was of a mixed humour. Penny was excellent company. We chatted in the Bostonian Eatery whilst the alcohol flowed. Sadly we were drinking foul tasting Retsina, a liquid that the Greeks mysteriously refer to as wine. Understandable of course because we were in a Greek restaurant, a country not famous for its cuisine. Coming from a Brit I know that's quite a statement so I prodded my starter (something awful wrapped in vine leaves) sullenly around my plate and concentrated on enjoying the discourse. The owner proudly told us that we were in a completely authentic Greek environment to which I inquired, "Does that mean we can't drink the water?" A remark that went down as well as a French kiss at a family reunion. Notwithstanding this I had the remarkable and unusual experience of eating a Moussaka without finding a pubic hair in it...there's a first time for everything.

The other bizarre thing about the place was the washroom. There was a condom machine on the wall which only sold items in Kiwi Fruit flavour. I ruminated that maybe this was a purely Greek phenomenon and speculated no further as I wasn't planning to buy any. I've always had a challenging relationship with condoms. I recall the stumbling awkward ritual of buying them over the counter in Chemists in seventies Britain. A regular occurrence as I was in my very early teens and I and my pier group were at it like rabbits...i.e. we ate carrots all the time...which was about as close we all got for a while.

I remember once going to Soviet Russia before the wall came down (quite an experience) and the British authorities provided me with a list of do's and don'ts, one of which stated sombrely 'You are advised to take your condoms with you as opposed to buying them locally due to quality issues'. Sound advice I thought but then that led me to think, "How many is enough?" I thought it would be pathetic if I took only three but would it be outrageously optimistic (or even arrogant) to take more? As it happens I took twelve and used none of them...so much for positive thinking! In retrospect it could have been something to do with the fact that the county was so God awful I spent most of the evenings drowning in Vodka. The result of this consumption was a set of reproductive equipment which was about as much use as an ashtray on a motorbike. Anyway, I digress...yet again.

Despite the standard of the lunch, which was even less enjoyable than Shakespearian Comedy improv (yes, such a dreadful thing exists...be warned), the standard of the company was outstanding. To say that Penny was a roller coaster hard wired totally committed 'spank head' would be like calling World War Two a 'minor altercation'. Compared to her I merely had a passing interest and yet I'd obviously piqued hers. Within half an hour of leaving me Hanna had been on the phone giving her a (literally) blow-by-blow account of the proceedings. She'd pressed Hanna for details and demanded to know every nuance of the session. I hadn't yet realised there was a spanking 'jungle telegraph' and my scene with Hanna had set the wires trembling...or was it the drums sounding? Anyway, the word was out.

Penny was early thirties, extraordinarily bright and a lawyer (another one) and possessed of what can best be described as a robust sense of humour. This humour had been honed to a razor sharp point by years of serial 'frog kissing' before she finally got where she needed to go. Her legion stories included numerous nervous tops, first timers who'd lied about their experience, no shows, figgers (remember the ginger root?), guys seeking sexual favours and on one memorable occasion a man so big that he'd have probably been refused employment by airport security...difficult to believe I know. If indeed men are from Mars and women are from Venus then Penny was definitely from much further afield, probably somewhere even the Hubble telescope would have difficulty locating, hence the fact that 'Planet Spank' has not yet been discovered. I liked her enormously.

Her most recent toe curling howler had involved her unknowingly pocket dialling her boss moments before being extensively beaten. He'd heard everything. A difficult one to come back from I mused but she just brushed it off with an infectious giggle.

As we enjoyed our post repast coffees Jeanine came striding into the restaurant. Five foot eleven of Italian attitude in flat shoes. A striking example of femininity she was one of the very few people to exemplify, that yes, it is indeed possible to spend too much time at the gym. She fumed at the late arrival of her luggage. She sat down at our table spitting venom at the airline and hinting at legal ramifications that would have given the most hardened of defence attorney's sleepless nights. She was altogether less formidable later in the afternoon when I'd given her her final cane stroke. Her pugnacious attitude long gone after a protracted series of thrashings that had shown both her and Penny to have an almost inexhaustible appetite for discipline. And they looked good in schoolgirl uniforms as well. The best of times. I immediately christened her 'Juiced Jeanine'.

That evening, as I insouciantly puffed contentedly on a poor quality cigar, much conversation ensured and numerous war stories were swapped. Penny revealed herself to be very much a doyenne of the domestic discipline world and it appeared only the players she approved of made it to her inner circle of spankers and spankees. She recommended people to other people and 'put people together' on literally a global basis. She leaned across and gently patted me on the cheek. "And you," she said, "Are in!" It felt like being inducted into the mafia. What awaited me if I broke the rules? Would I wake up with the head of one of Chloe's parrots in the bed…or even worse?

She then provided me with a list of at least a dozen women in the Manhattan area that would want to play with me immediately. At that moment my Blackberry chirped with an incoming email. Yet another response to my post, the fifth that week. The dam was beginning to break. This was all getting a little out of hand. For the uninitiated reading this, yes there really are as many kinky women out there as men and that's official.

Our conversations and exchanges went on into the evening. As the wine flowed they both talked enthusiastically of the experiences that they'd had and they hoped to have in the future. They talked of 'pushing their boundaries' and 'expanding their limits'. Jeanine bemoaned the fact that she'd never played with 'A truly cruel woman', a comment that I took note of for future reference. Her last 'frog kissing' episode was mercifully quite some time previously. It had involved a long and exciting exchange of emails with a Harvard professor who wrote both eloquently and intensely of his experiences and 'things to come'. Eventually they'd arranged to meet in a café to test the waters. Highly motivated she'd arrived at the appointed place on time and was disappointed to note that the only person in the establishment was a mortally pungent apparently homeless person huddled in the corner. He looked up and said, "Are you Jeanine?"

Towards the very latter part of the evening Jeanine started to demonstrate an appetite and capacity for alcohol that would have made an English rugby team look inadequate. The drunker she got the louder she got and, appallingly, the more affectionate she got. By the end of the night both Penny and I felt that we were entertaining an Amazonian Goddess who had been deprived of male company for several lifetimes. A good night coffee was refused and an enquiry made as to the liquors' available. Penny apologised. All she had in the apartment was a nauseating five-year-old bottle of Banana Liqueur, an unwanted gift that was understandably gathering dust. "That'll do," Jeanine enthused. Oh dear. I heard distant warning bells.

Jeanine and I eventually departed to our nearby hotel. I poured her into the elevator and entered my hotel room well pleased with the day's events. Five minutes or so later there was a knock on my door. I opened it and Jeanine fell through carrying two cans of beer. Beer? "It's all I could get," she breathed.

She then waxed lyrical about her last boyfriends many inadequacies (him being a non kinkster was one of them) and had me squirming with revelations about his sexual technique or rather the lack of it. She loudly bemoaned the fact that he'd disapproved of her recently pierced nipples and with that she whisked off her t-shirt to solicit my opinion. Narrowly avoiding being poked in the eye I offered muted approval of the display. She then wandered off to the bathroom leaving me wondering if I had stumbled into the fourth dimension. I stared out of the window into the night sky looking for deliverance.

A tap on my shoulder brought me out of my reveries. I turned to see her standing stark naked. "Do you think my abdominals are too muscular?" she asked. "For Gods sake," I blustered. I confess that the flesh was willing but experience counselled clearer thinking. Consequences, there's always consequences. A moment later I was living, albeit briefly, in another world. It was Jeanine world. I say Jeanine world, as she seemed to be everywhere. Her mouth was planted to mine like a sink plunger and no matter where I reached out part of her seemed to be there. It was like trying to extract myself from a steroid driven Italian octopus with rampaging hormones. Actually, she *was* a steroid driven Italian octopus with rampaging hormones. My attempts to hold her off were as effective as trying to halt a herd of charging buffalo with a leaky water pistol.

I may have briefly blacked out due to lack of oxygen and when I came to, wobbling uncertainly against the end of the bed, my shirt was long gone and my trousers were about to be a mere memory. I took the direct approach and stood forcefully on her toe. Ungentlemanly I know but it was the only way I could think of bringing matters to halt without her loosing too much face. It had the desired affect insomuch as her ardour was immediately and loudly quenched. With a pout she left. I met her briefly the next morning in the breakfast room where she was nursing a hangover so bad I almost felt sorry for her. The incident was never mentioned again. Hey, we're all human, though I was never really quite sure if Jeanine was.

Chapter Ten

Settling in

I looked around at the buildings surrounding me and attempted to drink in their seemingly aching provenance. This was living history American style. In the UK I'd had dust on my desk older than these dwellings but to a New Yorker they were ancient. I stood there with my bag of tricks and momentarily considered this and then wondered how much kink was actually going on in Sutton Place. However much there was, there was very shortly going to be some more. Actually there was going to be a lot more than even I could have ever imagined…and I can imagine quite a bit.

Trudy had come storming through my well set up defences in a manner that would have had the defensive line of the New York Jets nervously stepping back a pace. Her gushing enthusiasm for 'matters eclectic' was demonstrated by an endearing laugh on the telephone, a spectacular photograph indicating a delightful half hidden visage and an even more delightful body topped off with a list of delicious fantasies to titillate even the most jaded kinkster. And she hadn't done anything yet! I'd acquiesced to see a newbie purely from the quality of her obvious and genuine enthusiasm.

Eschewing the option of a 'get to know each other dinner' at a neutral venue she'd suggested we meet at her place and eat there. Curiosity had got the better of me and I agreed. Now, standing in front of the building that housed her apartment, I found my normal habit of regarding opulence with disdain difficult to affect. What the hell did this woman do for a living? Unless she was a professional lottery winner I failed to understand how a thirty three year old could maintain such an existence. Even if I doubled my salary I thought it unlikely I could even handle the monthly service fees for such a place.

As I battled my way through the almost ankle deep carpet towards the concierges desk I was sharply reminded of my own humble beginnings. An existence who's sole high point was on a Sunday when my mother would remove the whalebone from her corset and boil it up for a broth. We couldn't even afford butter. To compensate we kept a pig out in the back garden which we used to chase around until it sweated then rubbed bread on its back. Things changed of course. I'd clawed my way up the greasy corporate pole and, having slid down it again twice, once almost to the very bottom, I currently desperately gripped on to it firmly just above the midway point and counted my blessings. Whalebone broth was now long behind me but caviar and champagne was still not yet a daily event.

On the lofty heights of the God knows what floor I sought out her apartment. I couldn't believe how far away the different apartment entrances were from each other. I found the correct number and rang the bell. Half a minute later the door was opened by an extremely attractive dark haired woman deliciously dressed as a maid. 'Blimey,' I thought, 'No messing around here. Straight into the action.' "Hello Trudy, "I grinned as I walked over the threshold. "Great outfit." The woman gave me an odd look. "I'm not Trudy," She said, "She's waiting for you in the lounge." I blushed and cringed simultaneously and followed the genuine maid through the palatial apartment to meet with the actual Trudy. Considering the quality of the domain I was surprised to be startled by two plump rats scuttling rapidly across my path. Dogs, or so I was informed. I wasn't totally convinced.

Unsurprisingly the real Trudy looked more like her photograph than the maid. She greeted me effusively with a squeeze and a couple of over dramatic air kisses and bade me welcome. I naturally accepted her kind offer of a drink and yes, a large one would go down very nicely indeed thank you. The maid said goodbye for the evening after unpacking some delivered nibbles and Trudy and I locked our horns in conversation. Actually that's not quite true, I had difficulty in getting a word in edgeways. "You know," she breathed, "I want to try everythang." No that wasn't a spelling mistake, that's how she really talked.

'Everythang', to me was the word of an enthusiast but only a potential enthusiast. As we've ascertained there's a distinct difference. Further questioning revealing this interest was a very recent phenomenon. A friend had recommended 'The Story of O' which she'd devoured in a single sitting and then she'd gone on to devour a lot more since, an awful lot more. It was about this time I noticed next to some very nice pieces of Thai art there were a number of photographs adorning the sides featuring a pale young man, photos which revealed two things about him. a) He had a penchant for Comme de Garcon shorts and b) he was in the Navy. "That's Clarke," she said, "My boyfriend." I was about to venture the very obvious comment concerning the nature of our rendezvous when she added. "It/s OK, he's totally cool with this."

Evidently 'Cool Clarke' was currently at sea serving aboard the aircraft carrier *USS Enormous* and would not be back for two months. Well, for obvious reasons, as far as I was concerned, this was a very good thing. Looking at the spindly specimen in the photos I couldn't quite work out their connection, a point which I queried. "Oh," she offered, "He's very smart." Hmm smart enough to let his girlfriend indulge in this sort of activity whilst he was off protecting the free world. Clearly the eponymous Clarke was either an enlightened man or he wasn't that smart. I never found out which. Two weeks later he was yesterday's news as Trudy's proclivity for investigating kink expanded exponentially whilst I raced to keep up. In the meantime I was grateful for his laudable sacrifices in helping to keep me safe from my enemies and I was even more grateful he wasn't around.

Her father, a man who was apparently one of those people who had 'The Second' or 'The Third' after his name, had set up a Trust Fund so enormous Trudy had to work overtime just to try and spent the interest on the interest. I was aware of his company and told her so. "Really," she said, "You know, even though he's the Chairman, Daddy still works so hard. He still insists on going on buying trips himself. He brings me back those wonderful Thai pieces." This was strange considering I knew none of his product range originated in Thailand. I strongly suspected there was some other compelling reason he regularly visited the rocket polishing capital of the world, but I didn't speculate out loud. Anyway, notwithstanding the gargantuan amount of cash 'Trust Fund Trudy' had, she was intelligent and her international education showed. Work for her was assisting in fund raising for various charities, endeavours that met with my wholehearted approval.

After braving the onslaught of excruciatingly detailed descriptions as to what she thought she wanted to do and what she wanted to know more about, I endeavoured to rein in her enthusiasm a tad. I'd barely opened my mouth when she saw my goodie bag. "Are those your toys?" she gushed and unzipped it. She ohhed and ahhed at the various implements, examining each one painstakingly whilst barraging me with questions. As with so many who discover kink a little later in life she was exploding out of the cupboard with the power of a moderately sized nuclear device. I think I did 'Cool Clarke' a favour. Facing the Taliban and Al Queda was probably preferable (and easier to deal with) than what he would have faced from Trudy upon his return home.

"Would you like to see my toy selection?" she said. Not giving me a chance to reply she practically manhandled me into her sumptuous bedroom and dramatically flung open one of the wardrobes. Immediately, a veritable tsunami of battery operated plastic penises flooded out like a burst water main. "Opps," she said, "Wrong wardrobe." I waded out of the vibrator mountain and followed her to the next door. This she opened with a flourish. It was like being back in Leatherman.

"I've been ordering stuff online," She offered. Indeed she had. A collection of fetish clothing and accoutrement confronted me that a top of the range Pro Domme would have envied. You name it, it was there, including a significant representation from the 'Cock and Ball Torture" sector of the market. Yes, I'd definitely done 'Cool Clarke' a big favour. I was stunned at the variety and even more stunned at what she must of spent. I affected a semblance of nonchalance for about five seconds. "Jesus Trudy," I exclaimed, "You don't even know if you really like any of this stuff."

She giggled (very attractively I have to say) and, unasked, stripped to a thong "I'm going to find out now though aren't I?" she laughed. I say 'thong'. In reality it was so insignificant I couldn't decide whether to remove it or floss my teeth with it. I studied her body with abject appreciation. She was as fit as a butcher's dog (which, if you're a Brit, means very fit indeed!).

I opted to conduct an 'introductory' session. Simply giving her the opportunity to feel what each implement was like. A gentle way of easing her into that which she was convinced she was going to enjoy. It appeared she'd convinced herself correctly. She squealed, laughed, swore and chuckled as I worked my way through the items. An hour later she lay face down on the bed displaying a beautifully red rear. She looked at me with a florid face. "That was great. Can we do some other stuff now?" I couldn't help but laugh. She'd certainly hit her stride. I pulled some rope and feather from my bag then plugged in my tazer and went to work. I was joking about the feather.

I initially chalked Trudy up as a success. Yes, we'd certainly meet again soon I assured her as I left and no she couldn't top me later. Could she top me at some time in the future she'd enquired? I considered this for but a nanosecond and replied "Most certainly. When hell freezes over and we're all invited to the skating party." I received a pout for my observations but a good-natured one. By this time my mind was turning to other matters. The need to assuage my bottoming proclivities was beginning to manifest itself again with a vengeance and there was about to be a window of opportunity in my vanilla existence. This would allow me to indulge.

At the time I was dating a woman who had a capacity for alcohol that staggered the imagination. Now don't misunderstand me, getting drunk is most certainly one of life's great experiences, unless of course you're a glass of water, but this women could have made the national drinking team. She only ever drank on Friday and Saturday evenings but good God could she put it away. Apart from this slight aberration in character she was an appallingly clean living type who exercised like a demon. She would think nothing of getting up at five in the morning and running ten miles. I didn't think very much of it either. The result of this frenzied activity meant she had the continence of an ox. I can remember many a Friday trying to speak through a fog of alcohol whilst she communicated with seemingly no ill effects from the huge quantities of drink she'd managed to put away. The evenings always seemed to end the same way with me blundering up her staircase bouncing off the walls murmuring, "Be gentle with me."

The other memorable thing about her was that for some bizarre reason she had nylon sheets, which was something to do with a cotton allergy. The downside of this was continual toenail snagging and the resultant static electricity caused by any nocturnal 'activity'. Many was the time where there were sparks and cracks which I'd like to claim where down to the quality of my performance but sadly were due to physics. Moisture attracts and conducts electricity. There were occasions when I leapt from the sheets squealing like a pig. Initially she thought I was in the throws of ecstasy but the smell of burning eventually convinced her that she was not seeing passion but pain. I will say no more save for the fact that a condom was essential as rubber is a good insulator. Anyway, exit visas were being arranged so later that evening, with admirably restrained prose, I wrote a note to Domme Jackeline.

She wrote back promptly saying, "I'd be happy to see you again. Shall I plan for an hour or a self indulgent two?" Oh she was good, very very good.

I put my lascivious anticipation back behind locked doors and considered my situation. It really was all going swimmingly. Sure I'd 'skinned my knees' to start with but this persistence thing was certainly working. Thanks to the Machiavellian machinations of 'Pernicious Penny' and my own postings I now had a supply of supplicants which exceeded even my own outrageous appetites and with Domme Jackeline I could attend to my other proclivities. There was now most definitely enough kink in my life…wasn't there? With that I took down my Internet 'ad' and looked forward to meeting Celeste, the final woman to pass muster before I took down my post.

I don't normally have much time for fascists but Celeste was my sort of fascist insomuch as she was a gym Nazi. Like 'Juiced Jeanine' she worked out fanatically but without the added benefit of pharmaceutical assistance and with less emphasis on weights. Her supremely trim and lithe figure was clearly evident through her well-chosen outfit and I approved. I approved very much indeed. With her shock of dirty blond hair, finely defined facial features and sharp tongue, the package she presented was most entertaining. She carried her Jewish guilt with an outrageous aplomb which was laudable in the extreme and most amusing. She also had one of the darkest senses of humour I'd ever encountered. A few months hence I called her during Passover. When the phone answered I loudly declared 'Happy Jew Day' to which there was a stunned silence. Her Grandmother had picked up the phone.

Like many she'd had her share of wretched experiences and had even been very occasionally involved with the New York 'scene' on its outermost fringes. Seeing me cringe at such a reference she declined to venture further information. Up until that time I liked my play private. Even though we played with our little group of like-minded aficionados back in the day we were an extremely private bunch, an aspect to our interactions that had always sat very well with me.

Upon meeting she questioned me sharply (but intelligently) on my experience and realised very quickly that it significantly exceeded her own. Her main thing was discipline and her ultimate fantasy was the single tail. The evening was panning out rather well. I understood why for her single tail was still only a fantasy. She mirrored my own view insomuch as there are very few people who know how to use the damn thing. To my chagrin Chloe had once insisted on showing me a number of Internet clips featuring this activity and I'd been beyond appalled at the lack of technique. Frightening stuff. Almost as frightening was the physical condition of the men I'd seen on the receiving end. They seemed to have been selected for their moment of stardom by their ability to impersonate beached whales. Their pasty blubber rolled and their jowls jiggled as their sagging bodies endured the numbingly bad application of this most sophisticated of implements. Yuck! For me, kink should be elegant and beautiful. This wasn't.

In fairness to most Pro Dommes I cannot be too critical per se. I was to find out in the professional scene that single tail was very much a minority request and consequently for most of these dominants, it simply wasn't worth the time to undertake the enormous practice needed to master it. When I'd played previously I was the main single tailer in our little enclave of enthusiasts having learned the basics from Stacy. Even 'German Julia', whose dominance and skill sets I very much respected, or indeed my ex s/o whose own abilities were almost at the same level, were simply not even close to being up to par with the implement. I wouldn't let anyone near me with the thing and, as a result, I'd never experienced it myself.

Not only did I share Celeste's fear of bad practitioners I also shared her fantasy. To be strung up naked and single tailed in a real dungeon by a beautiful and genuinely sadistic leather clad Dominatrix. For me it would represent the ultimate challenge and visual image. Would I have what it took? Would it ever happen? Could I ever find such a person? And, really, shouldn't I have more important things in my life to aspire to? Well it was now certainly going to happen for Celeste although it wouldn't be with a dominatrix, it would be with me, and I didn't even own a pair of leather chaps! I resolved to do nothing whatsoever about this shortfall. I may be generalising but when it comes to men wearing fetish gear, with the very occasional notable exception, there's a very thin line indeed between looking like a dick and looking like a total dick.

I contemplated the outstanding prospect of whipping Celeste's motivational physique. I could already visualise it. The atmosphere, the lighting, what sort of music I'd use. One could think about this sort of thing way too much. A few days later however I wasn't thinking about it at all. The only thing on my mind was survival.

Domme Jackeline had listened attentively to my proscribed fantasy scenario. She'd nodded sagely when I emphasised certain aspects which were crucial to me and murmured understandingly when I described their importance. She then totally ignored everything I'd said and bade me strip and once again put my nose against the wall. There was something in her manner that made it impossible for me to venture a protestation. Oh yes, true dominance, that was it. She enquired in a threatening tone, "Are you scared?" No one had ever asked me that before. Well, I wasn't going to say 'yes' was I? I didn't want to be a total wuss. "I am understandably concerned," I replied, trying unsuccessfully to add an edge of sarcasm. She pushed my nose into the wall and repeated, "I said are you sacred?" I swallowed. "No," I replied defiantly. "That," she hissed, "Is because you lack imagination." For a moment there was a stony silence. "I'm going to give you the thrashing of your life," she whispered. Christ...who the hell was this bloody woman?

A short while later I didn't care who she was. The only thing I cared about was making sure I absolutely never did this again. Forgoing any warm up whatsoever she'd positioned me on the bed and had gone to work with a brutal rubber strap which had me yelling out loud at every impact. No one had ever hit me so hard...with an emphasis on the word 'ever'. Whilst trying to endure the beating I marvelled at her skill. Intensity and accuracy are a notoriously difficult balance and yet not a stroke was off target. No wraps, nothing too high or to low. She really knew what she was doing. She built to a stage where I was a heartbeat away calling a stop to things then eased of momentarily then came back even harder, punctuating her strokes with occasional admonishments and instructions "Head down," "Don't move your legs." "Raise your bottom up higher," Her voice pitch perfect. Commanding yet not haranguing and certainly never a hint of hesitation. I lost count of the number of blows.

She switched to a heavy leather strap, a thickness of which I'd never seen before and brought it down so ferociously I almost screamed. "Shhhh," she breathed, "Take the pain." Her voice pierced my very being. I knew I'd take it. I'd take it for her. The pumping endorphins once again allowing me to slip into the fantasy. God knows how many strokes later I lay exhausted and finished. She once again applied ice cubes and I luxuriated in their coolness. The all too brief respite was interrupted by her inquiring "How many cane strokes did I give you last time?" A chilling sense of 'déjà vu' overcame me. This wasn't even vaguely funny. I found it difficult to speak but I eventually managed to form the words "Seventy." She promptly gave me one hundred and fifty. During their application she once again admonished but she also soothed and encouraged. The soothing and encouragement was a head messing experience. She made me feel I was lucky to be there. Equally as perverse was the fact it was during the soothing that she hit me hardest. It was the most thrilling session I'd ever had. In the last few strokes I'd managed to get a brief glace at her in the mirror as she swung away. Yes, there it was, undeniably in her eyes… savagery.

When it was all over and I was able to finally communicate like a normal human being I voiced my thoughts. How did she know this was what I wanted when I didn't even know myself this was the type of session I craved? How had she managed to read me and get me to take more than I'd ever taken before? She smiled an enigmatic smile. "Because I'm a real Dominatrix," she said, "It's who I am." Yes she was, of that there was no doubt. Beautiful, truly cruel and sadistic and yet almost clinically safe in her application. Perfection. When not playing she was cool, intelligent, witty and composed. When playing…she actually scared me. A delicious fear which was complemented by her inordinate attention to safety. A flawless combination. I summoned up my courage and tentatively ventured the inquiry, "Can you single tail?"

Chapter Eleven

Where the Wild Things Are

Unsurprisingly Jackeline said she could, and so could I as 'Single Tail Celeste' found out shortly afterwards. She'd secured a private play place in midtown where she finally came to experience that about which she had always fantasised and was not disappointed. Neither was I. With embarrassingly inevitable (but totally appropriate) Gregorian Chants resonating solemnly in the background, she'd stripped in the dim candle light with a delicious shiver and a discernable nervousness. Minutes later her arms were fastened above her head and her ankles were held apart by a spreader bar, her sinuous body now an X shape in front of me, a study of beauty and submission. The first stroke saw her arch her back and I drank in the stark definition of her superbly refined muscle tone. I had rarely seen anything so exquisite.

Exquisite was not a word I'd use to describe the next person I would meet in a kink encounter though I'd certainly employ the epithet 'striking'. Celeste had been invited to a private fetish gathering and, insisting I'd enjoy it, suggested we go together. I immediately declined. The ensembles we'd had back in the day were immensely private. No one attended who hadn't been vetted and jumped though hoops and that was the way I liked it. There were no cretins or creeps. They were all in shape intelligent professional types who had come together through diligence, effort and a sincere appreciation of their erotic inclinations. She indignantly countered by asking why this get together would be any different. I protested, demurred, procrastinated and made awkward foppish Hugh Grant like mannerisms and almost stamped my feet. I emphatically indicated it really wasn't my thing and there wasn't a chance in hell I'd ever attend such a soiree. I made my point abundantly plain and told her I would hear no more on the matter. One has to lay down the law sometimes.

Arriving together at the party the following weekend, the door was opened by a most memorable image. Clad in the most beautifully made body hugging black corset, together with thigh high scarlet laced leather boots (with six inch heels) was a man. I was momentarily speechless, an event as rare as Panda sushi. Actually, whilst it's not my gig I've got to say, he looked great and good for him. Whilst rooted to the spot in surprise, a woman, also resplendent in leather, squeezed past me into the enclave towing a further woman on a leash behind her dressed as a schoolgirl. "Oh Heaven," purred the slave, "They've got a cage." They did too. As 'Trust Fund Trudy' would have said, they had 'everythang'.

The hostess was a professional domme of some repute whom I recognised from when I was doing my research. Resplendent in figure hugging latex, she bade Celeste and I a gracious welcome in a distinctive Southern drawl then moved on to attend to yet more new arrivals. The venue was obviously where she plied her trade as the accoutrement of the business were everywhere, together with the aforesaid cage in which the schoolgirl slave now reposed. Business must be good I concluded. The array of BDSM paraphernalia was most impressive as was the size of the playspace. To my distress Celeste promptly vanished into the crowd of leather and rubber clad partyites leaving me feeling distinctly less than comfortable. I knew no one though I did recognise a further couple of faces from my initial 'Domme research'. So, I concluded...this was where the wild things were...

I vowed to stay both inconspicuous and innocuous until I found my feet and retrieved my long forgotten kink etiquette. To accomplish this I meandered over to a burgeoning buffet where I seized a cold bottle of US branded beer. Drinking American beer is much like making love close to a canal, i.e. it's fucking close to water but as I wanted to keep a clear head I felt it an appropriate beverage. I wanted to sip on it nonchalantly whilst I cast my critical eye over the assembled personage and then ease myself into the fray whilst not attracting too much attention.

To assuage a momentary pang of hunger I seized a Dorito and plunged ii into a dip whilst I continued to scan the scene. I bit down and felt my mouth explode from a searing heat of the hottest Taco sauce I'd ever experienced this side of the border. In an uncontrolled reflex reaction I spat the offending article out loudly, spraying the air with a fine cloud of Dorito crumbs causing consternation from those closest to me. In a blind panic, seeking to quench the fire in my throat, I frantically grabbed for my cold beer, knocking sundry condiments noisily to the floor as I did so. I put the bottle to my lips and gulped. In my indecent haste I managed to lodge some foil from the cap into one of my ancient fillings. It felt like someone drilling for oil in my gum. I shrieked loudly, leapt up and tried to stop myself banging my head on the table with the pain.

And so was my low-key introduction into the New York kink scene.

Some time later, once I'd eventually managed to lower my embarrassment screens a few inches and peek carefully over the top, I summoned up the courage to mingle. To my abject horror I literally bumped into 'Mistress who didn't know the names of her own implements' teetering uncertainly on high heels. Incredibly and wonderfully she didn't recognise me, which says a lot about the sort of impression I generally make. Cleary 'tired and emotional' she launched into a conversation of such stupefying inanity I was almost thinking about retreating back to the Mexican dip but politesse necessitated I endure her tiresome warbling. She finished her oratory with "Well I've always regarded myself as special." Biting back the bile I sharply offered, "Well I'm glad to hear that. I wouldn't have wanted you to think you were any different from the rest of us." Well really! This gave her a moment of pause. You could see the cogs grinding away. "What I mean is," she said, "Is no one ever tells me anything I don't know." I resisted the urge to explain you need to have a vocabulary of more than fifty words for people to communicate anything of value to you but I stopped myself. I recalled the wise observation from someone or other who said, "If you can't be honest at least have the decency to be vague." I had the decency to be vague. I did however leave her with something to cogitate on. "Actually," I said, "I'm pretty special myself. You know that product 'I can't believe it's not Butter'? Well, I can believe it's not butter."

My next encounter was with an incongruous representation of the male gender. A louche dullard adorned with more trinkets than an octogenarians mantelpiece who ventured a critique of the background music, explaining he had a passion for Jazz. And you wonder why I'd avoided fetish parties. I declined to vent my feelings fully on jazz for fear of causing friction. Taking my silence as encouragement he confessed that free form jazz explorations were enough to send him into ecstasy. Achieving Nirvana through musical masturbation eh? I had no idea the diminished chord was so powerful. I continued biting my tongue until he revealed that he was an accomplished tuba player. Well someone has to be I suppose. This revelation stunned me. I can understand deeply unattractive spotty teenage boys feverishly learning rock guitar. They were generally correct that competency in such an instrument would increase their chances with the opposite sex. Unless I'm missing something I seriously doubt if competency on the tuba has the same effect. I'm sure the same can be said of most brass instruments and probably the entire woodwind section of an average orchestra. I decided to bring our musically oriented conversation to a logical conclusion. I ventured that I'd been reliably informed a true gentleman was someone who can play the bagpipes but chooses not to. Never a truer word spoken.

Having left my mark, with a sprightly step and my spirits up, I moved on to create mayhem in other conversational groups. I was standing next to a posse of women, one of whom was bemoaning the fact she had had difficulty finding a boyfriend of late. She sighed and self mockingly laughed to her friends "Maybe I'm no good in bed." Unable to resist I piped up "That's not true, loads of people have told me you're great." The resulting intimidating silence necessitated my moving to another group where a handsome looking woman, resplendent in rubber, was bemoaning the fact at fifty-five sex was not what it was. Ever eager to solicit warmth and understanding I offered "I've always found older women are better in the sack because they think they may be doing it for the last time"....well I was trying to be supportive but in truth it wasn't received all that well. A dark chuckle behind me in response to my comment had me turning. A wicked smile greeted me. A wicked smile that I was to discover was sported by Mistress Angelique.

I'd recognised the hostess of the affair, Lady Sophie, as she'd shown her face on her website. I also knew enough to know she was a 'name' in NYC. Mistress Angelique I found out was regarded with equal reverence. I also recalled her website. Beautifully and intelligently written with not even a hint of a facial shot. So this is what she looked like. An elfin like face and a body clad not in leather, but in an enormously tasteful simple black loose fitting one-piece dress. A most pleasing visual experience. Her conversation and demeanour were equally agreeable. Sharp, educated and challenging. Oh, and as she'd laughed at my quip I modestly concluded she had an excellent sense of humour. She observed it appeared this type of gathering was an unusual experience for me. I confirmed this was indeed the case in recent years. I admitted the last time I'd seen so many people living in a fantasy world, wearing silly costumes and talking rubbish was a recent TV documentary I'd viewed on the Vatican. She laughed at my purported lack of tolerance. "Hey," I said, "Do I *look* like a people person?"

I did my level best to exude a raffish countenance and tried not to put my foot in my mouth too often. With Angelique it was an unnecessary effort. She was as real as it gets and God help you if she thought you were trying to be otherwise. We talked interests and persuasions. She asked offhandedly about my own and listened patiently as I detailed my very modest tally of proclivities. She responded likewise with a tally that could be described in many ways but certainly not as 'modest'. She laughed out loud at my facial reactions to the descriptions of some of her activity. She also got me up to speed on some of the website terms which had stumped me. Actually, now understanding what some of them were, I'd have rather remained ignorant. All in all she was a breath of fresh air and a much needed re education.

We ascertained that we both enjoyed administering the single tail. She listened patiently whilst I held forth with my strident and dogmatic views on the subject. Strident views which I aired without giving her the courtesy of an economy of words. At that moment another singularly attractive woman approached. "Oh," she said, "You like single tail? Angelique is pretty much the most skilled exponent in the business." I flushed while Angelique once again affected her hearty laugh. The two women clearly knew each other well, a fellow pro domme who I was also to find out was one of New York's finest. This was clearly a fairly elite gathering. With the notable exception of 'Mistress who doesn't know the name of her own implements' of course.

The new arrival, Domme Melissa, a tall willowy auburn haired dynamo, had apparently come to secure my assistance. "I'm going to pick up some more wine," she said, "I need a man to help me carry it, and you're it." And with that I left for the liquor store wondering with some annoyance what had happened to Celeste. We chatted as we promenaded down the street. "I heard you talking to Angelique about single tail," she said, "I make internet videos. You should let me single tail you in one. You wouldn't even have to pay me." I responded there were only two chances of that happening. No chance and absolutely no chance at all.

Upon our return Angelique strode over. "I'm going to do a single tail demo," she said "Are you up for it?" "I think not," I replied thoughtfully as I espied the absent Celeste across the room. "But," I added slowly, "I know someone who is." A short while later a mortified Celeste was once again being strung up to face the lash. The ensemble hushed and parted to allow Angelique some room and, with that, she began.

I have never before or since seen such a display of skill with a whip. As she demonstrated the most exquisite exhibition of throws (whip strokes) she moved around with an elegance that took my breath away. Someone described her as 'A ballet dancer with whips', which is an analogy I can resolutely confirm. I'd always regarded good kink scenarios as almost an art form. Angelique's display demonstrated that it indeed was and she was the maestro applying the brushstrokes. Whilst Celeste twitched and writhed under the assault Angelique shadowed and stalked her, sometimes pushing and sometimes pulling back, always in motion. There was such an intense energy exchange it was palpable. One of her friends said almost in shock "Angelique, I can feel you all the way over here." We all felt the same. I was aware I was watching something truly special. Incredibly, when it was all over and the exhausted Celeste was let down, she had barely a mark on her despite the twenty-minute ordeal. A master class indeed.

Chapter Twelve

Behind the Velvet Curtain

For me, Mistress Angelique, to whom I will always be sincerely grateful, turned out to be to overall kink connections what Pernicious Penny and Committed Chloe were to spanking and discipline connections. Of course Angelique knew copious quantities about the latter but she also knew a very great deal more about the former and embraced them wholeheartedly within her professional practice. When she wasn't plunging needles through some poor sods nipples, she was binding them in exquisite shibari (Japanese) bondage or doing wretched things to their genitals, sometimes all at the same time. Kink, as I've mentioned, is a very broad church and she enthusiastically embraced most of its numerous denominations.

At Lady Sophie's bash she'd kindly offered to assess my single tail technique and give me instruction. I was awash with gratitude and somewhat in awe of her skill. I jumped at the invitation. She bade me meet her at a fetish shop on the Lower

East Side where she had an errand to run. From there we'd grab a bite then depart to her studio. Thus, on a New York's summers day, enduring a humidity that can only normally be found in a hippopotamuses rectum, I found myself en route to Demask, a noted fetish store.

Espying the shop I quickly looked around to ensure Mark (or anyone else I knew) wasn't around, and ducked into the establishment. I was greeted by a pleasing air-conditioned coolness. In contrast a staff member offered an effusively warm welcome. She suggested I speak with her should I need any advice. Considering all I could see was a plethora of women's kink wear I wanted to state immediately for the record I wasn't a transvestite. Errr not that there's anything wrong with it of course but I felt the pressing need to set things straight. 'Straight' being the operative word. I didn't get a chance to open my mouth. From behind a cubicle at the side of the shop came a loud swearword and a voluminous cloud of talcum powder. There then followed some muffled grunts, yet more clouds of talcum power and a series of sounds reminiscent of someone strangling a cat.

A moment later a breathless Angelique stumbled out from behind the cubicle door, her face flushed, hair tousled and resplendent in a one-piece rubber bodysuit. "Godammit," she breathed, "That was a bitch to get on." And so it continued for the next half an hour until she was satisfied with her eventual choice. Whilst she laudably struggled and sweated to make her selection I mooched innocuously around the store. The range of women's clothing was quite fabulous. Leather, rubber and latex creations of exquisite quality abounded, some of outstandingly original design. Kink may be regarded as a minority occupation but it certainly attracts some very creative people. I murmured genuine approval.

Back at her stunningly well-equipped private studio she genteelly offered some piercing observations on my whip technique and set about trying to drag me up the skill sets ladder. She showed me throws I'd never seen or even thought of and patiently talked me through their execution. She set me practice rituals in order to refine my performance and solemnly outlined her own 'do's and don't' with the aforesaid implement. Stacy had been a competent single tailer, Angelique was a grand master.

In the preface I mentioned that amongst the ghastly dross there were true stars burning bright in the kink firmament. I was now beginning to meet them. 'Domme Jackeline' was most definitely one and so by fearsome reputation were Lady Sophie and Domme Mylissa. Angelique was also most certainly one. The pain, both metaphorical and physical, was beginning to pay off.

Angelique questioned me closely about my adventures with Chloe and the recipients I was rapidly collecting in my burgeoning coven. She was particularly curious about the whole concept of 'Domestic Discipline'. Of course she knew what it meant and she was no stranger to beating the living daylights out of people but our little 'niche within a niche' was something she wanted to investigate further. She asked if I could give a demonstration. I agreed immediately, knowing Chloe would be up for it in a heartbeat. Rubbing her hands together she enthused "Great. I'll invite Mistress Daphne over. She's got a real interest in this stuff." 'Mistress Daphne' had a formidable reputation, very formidable indeed. It would also mean me having to demonstrate my topping in front of two of its most feared practitioners! Mistress Daphne was yet another star in the firmament. The stars I'd met and the one I was now going to meet I eventually discovered represented the crème de la crème of New York Dominatrices. I eventually came to think of them as 'The Wild Bunch'.

I took my leave of Angelique, giving her plenty of time to prepare for the arrival of some corporate CEO. Apparently 'Ken', bless him, was still firmly locked into the eighties and dressed in what was best described as retro *Miami Vice* chique. I concurred with Angelique's view that these days the white suit, Gucci loafer look complete with a tight t-shirt is to be avoided. Equally it's important to have the sort of stomach whereby it's still possible to get a glimpse of your toes when you stand up. Evidently Ken was lamentably deficient in this area. It is at this stage I reminded myself of the valuable adage that one should keep ones words both soft and tender because tomorrow you may have to eat them.

The eponymous Kens orgasms had apparently been prevented for the last few weeks by use of a something called a 'chastity cage'. This device is locked onto the male genetalia and prevents erections. Why he would choose to pay for this privilege is a matter on which I cannot even begin to speculate. Why he'd also then want to have his scrotum stapled up and subjected to electric shocks is also a profound mystery. I queried this with Angelique. "Want?" she said in genuine amazement. "It's not about what he wants, it's about what I choose to do!" Err OK then. Fair enough. I thanked my instructor profusely for her time, shuddered and hit the streets.

As I made for the subway my phone vibrated pleasingly in my pocket. Not recognising the number I answered with some curiosity. "Gudday mate," an unfamiliar voice boomed. Whoever the caller was it appeared he'd had a foghorn surgically inserted into his throat at birth. "It's Frank," Searching around in the dusty recesses of my memory I found no evidence that I'd ever met a loud Australian man called Frank, though I'd met plenty of loud Australian men (all of them). "Penny told me to call you when I hit town," He continued, "She said we had a lot in common." He paused briefly for effect, "Are you with me mate?"

Well I certainly caught his drift but I politely pressed for clarification. Over familiarity is culturally uncomfortable for a Brit or as Domme Jackeline had eloquently referred to it, my 'Natural anal retentiveness'. A charming observation but definitely one with a spirit of truth I have to confess. I suddenly recalled a prior conversation with my Bostonian acquaintance. Frank, or 'Fanatical Frank' as I came to name him, was a Captain with one of Australia's major airlines. Whereas it's said sailors have a girl in every port, so did Frank, but he wasn't a sailor and he didn't romance them, he beat them.

We spoke for a while whist I held the phone a good two feet from my ear to stop any permanent hearing damage and as ever I found myself smiling at an Australians natural good humour. "Got a couple of right little chancers coming up to the hotel tonight," he enthused, "Come over this evening and blow the froth off a few and we'll take care of them together when they arrive." Well, I can't say he wasn't hospitable and I worked out that 'blowing the froth off a few' was Australian for drinking beer which is always a welcome activity. My evening's entertainment was set but I still had the afternoon to get through. At Chloe's request I was to meet up with a mysterious woman named Margaret.

Margaret was something of an enigma. A lawyer (yes yet another one) she'd advertised on Craigslist for a woman she could, well, dominate basically. Chloe reported the posting was clear and well thought through and had given her a genuine frisson of excitement. They'd exchanged thrilling little notes, which seemed to indicate Margaret's competent dominance and each exchange had further stimulated Chloe to push things forwards.

Eventually they'd met at a smart restaurant where her imperious yet considerate manner had found favour and they'd talked long into the afternoon. Nonetheless, when they'd parted company in the early evening Chloe was a mixed bag of emotions. The woman had certainly talked the talk and rang all her bells. She had however eventually revealed she was married with three kids and her husband knew nothing of this proposed activity. Strange but not unheard of. She'd then revealed she'd never done this before and that her 'master' had given her permission to do so.

Stamping on the brakes Chloe's warning antennae started twitching in an animated fashion. No the husband knew nothing of the 'master', it was only something she'd recently started, indeed she'd only very recently decided to indulge her fantasies after the nadir of her fortieth birthday. Despite her misgivings Chloe gave her the benefit of the doubt. Why? Because Margaret was attractive and intelligent and Chloe loved the idea of being topped by her. She could deal with the fact that Margaret had her own master as long as it didn't interfere with her own dynamic. Welcome to the 'wonderful world' of closet kinksters. Don't look for logic.

They agreed to meet again but by the time twenty-four hours had passed Margaret had called her three times asking intricate details of my own encounters with her, literally blow by blow accounts. She then said, "If I'm to take this forwards then I need to meet him (me)." At that point Chloe understood exactly where she was coming from and after she spoke to me so did I. We discussed it and as a favour to a friend I agreed to meet Margaret at my apartment. The woman called me. With total confidence in her voice she told me, "We need to talk about

Chloe and how she was going to deal with her." Yeah right! Dear me…talk about walking into the lion's den!

I met 'Fanatical Frank' that evening at an Irish bar close to his hotel. A huge man with a face only a mother could love. A startling beard, grown no doubt to unsuccessfully conceal more chins than a Chinese telephone directory, framed his wide grin. He looked more pirate than pilot. He greeted me with a bear hug which almost cracked a rib and pointed out two pints of Guinness on the bar. "They're yours mate," he bawled, "You've got catch up to do." Yes, I was definitely in the company of an Aussie. "Been looking forward to this evenings activities," He enthused, "It's all I could think of on the way down." No doubt his three hundred plus passengers would have been a mite surprised to know of the Captains thought processes during the tricky approach to JFK.

Frank had been a spanking enthusiast all his life "Since even before I grew hair I could sit on," he confessed. Though Australian he'd been sent to an all male British boarding school. "All Rugby, buggery and flogging," he murmured, "Still, one out of three ain't bad eh?" I nodded, having difficulty in actually managing to get a word into his good-natured onslaught. "Penny says you're alright," he continued, "So's she. Bit skinny though. I told her she was scrawnier than a cats cock." I considered this unique epithet as he pressed on. He told kink stories from the days when he'd been a fighter pilot in the Australian Air Force. I reacted with scepticism. "What?' He said, "You think they don't have kinksters in the military?" "No," I replied, "I didn't know you had an Air Force." He stopped in his tracks and gave me a hard stare then burst out laughing, "Yeah, you'll do!" and promptly ordered even more beer.

Sometime later we were in his palatial hotel room. In the bathroom two attractive giggling women were changing into school uniforms and Frank was laying out his implements. Kink and an excess of alcohol are an unsafe and problematic combination but not apparently for Frank. He had amazingly snapped back to total sobriety the moment the girls had arrived and behaved like a perfect gentleman. Sadly, as he held up one of his canes for my approval, I was convinced he was holding up at least two. Five pints of Guinness is a full four pints over my normal limit. Experience and consideration dictated I sit this one out and simply watch the events that were to transpire. Frank laughed. "Typical bloody Pom. Can't take his pop." I watched in blurred appreciation as he reached into his wardrobe and pulled out an immaculate black teachers gown. This was followed by a genuine mortarboard. He donned the outfit, sucked in his stomach and bellowed to the girls. "Ladies, I'm ready to punish you now." I fell into a beer-induced sleep on the extravagant sofa, numb to the squeals of his victims.

Previously that afternoon, Margaret had arrived at my apartment, a picture of elegant sophistication, with a confident manner and a weasel like dog who promptly peed on my carpet. Being British I laughed it off in affected nonchalance, practically blaming myself for fact she'd arrived with a bloody rodent on a leash. Allowing myself a scowl whilst I prepared coffee I was back to my normal beaming self when I returned to the lounge. When the pleasantries were over I indicated for her to ask what it was she wanted to ask. She calmly smoothed away some imaginary creases on her immaculate skirt and made to speak.

As she opened her mouth I deliberately butted in, "I understand you've got a master?" It was a statement. Put out of her stride she hesitated. "Yes," she said. "He's very severe," adding in a hushed voice, "Once he even used a wooden spoon on me." My gulp of coffee exploded through my nose.

When I'd cleaned myself up, with great difficulty I tried to give her my best sharp gaze. Flushing red, Margaret blustered, "Enough about me. I'm here to talk about Chloe." I stopped trying not to laugh about 'Master Wooden Spoon' and stared hard at her until she began to fidget uncomfortably. I spoke slowly and deliberately. "Don't insult my intelligence. I know exactly why you're here…and so do you." There was silence as we locked eyes. She held her breath.

"I want you to go into my bedroom and remove all of your clothes. When you've done so I want you to lie on the bed with a pillow under your waist so your bottom is totally accessible. I will come through in a moment and give you the punishment you deserve. Do I make myself clear?" You could have heard a mosquito cough. She stared back in apparent disbelief then, as Chloe and I had so rightly predicted she would, she meekly stood up and walked to the bedroom. I followed her in shortly afterwards and did what needed to be done and there wasn't a wooden spoon in sight. As I said, don't look for logic. Chloe and I affectionately christened her 'Muddled Margaret'.

The following morning my cell phone went off at an hour that can best be most charitably described as unsociable. It heralded the onslaught of my hangover, which, whilst not being the worst I'd ever had, would have nonetheless actually have registered on the Richter scale. Franks hundred-decibel Australian amiableness blasted from the receiver. "Sorry about the early call mate but I'm jetlagged. Did I wake you?" I grunted in confirmation. Unperturbed he continued unabated.

"Penny said you knew people, you know, dominants, here in the city." Dear God it was way too early to be talking about this stuff. To me kink is like alcohol. Anytime before noon just isn't right. "I do," was my terse response. "But getting yourself beaten in this town isn't hard, just go on the net," I urged, hoping he'd just bugger off and leave me to my headache. "That's not what I want," he said, "What I really want is…"

Five minutes later, ashen faced, I put down the phone with a quivering hand. Christ I hardly knew the guy and whilst I passed no judgement on his proclivities I really didn't need to hear about them at 7.30 in the bloody morning. Actually I didn't need to hear about them ever. This kink thing was getting a little out of hand. Time to pull back. Yup, I'd definitely take my foot off the accelerator and think about applying the brakes. Of course I'd still accompany Angelique as requested to the following weekends fetish bash but that would be it for a while. Oh, and also I'd arranged to be single tailed by Domme Jackeline. So, anyway, after those two things I'd hold up for a while. Well I most certainly would after my next planned rendezvous with Trust Fund Trudy. Damn, I'd also forgotten I'd promised to do a demo for Angelique and Daphne with Chloe. Well, I'd put the brakes on fairly soon anyway, really I would.

On the way to the aforementioned party Angelique offered, "I managed to find someone to sort out your friend by the way." Apparently there was no shortage of women in the city who, for a fee, were more than happy to ram a gloved fist up an affluent airline pilot's bottom. A fact I found surprising yet most unintriguing and resolutely unappealing. Thoughts I voiced a mite too vociferously. She laughed at my squeamishness. "You gotta learn to relax," she urged. Relaxed I was prepared to be but never relaxed enough to consider indulging in Franks chosen bent. "You know," she said, "There's actually more bacteria in our mouths than our backsides. "Well I knew which end I'd rather be kissing and if we were talking about Frank it wouldn't be either of them. No doubt he's one of these people who lays in bed at night hoping to be abducted by aliens. Personally I can't for the life of me understand why extra terrestrials would traverse the vastness of space simply to stick probes up the rear ends of lonely attention seekers. It's one of life's great mysteries I s'pose. A bit like why would a man want to do ballet? Or who becomes an accountant through choice? Or, more importantly, speed walking at the Olympics. What the fuck is that all about? And come to that, why would anyone want to voluntarily learn the bassoon? But I appear to have digressed again.

This was now my third such attendance at a private gathering and I moved through the affray in confidence and mixed easily with exotically dressed kindred spirits. At least that was the plan. The reality is I moved cautiously and felt my way very carefully, my kink radar still not yet fully refined. The key difference between these New York gatherings and the small private ones I used to attend were the presence of professional dommes and their acolytes and people who were evidently well known in the scene. I'd discovered, much to my surprise, that there was a distinct pecking order in evidence based on a whole manner of criteria. I was pleased to discover those with whom I was friendly (and who subsequently became good friends) were at the very top of the tree. This afforded me a credibility and provenance that would have been difficult to achieve otherwise. I had however no wish to be a 'scene guy', preferring the majority of my activity to be almost obsessively private and 'under the radar', however I cannot pretend I didn't enjoy these sporadic encounters enormously. In the main I got to meet a lot of interesting kinky people and on occasion, as is so true in real life, I also met people for whom the word 'interesting' was not even remotely applicable.

In amongst the throng at the appointed destination I listened attentively as Angelique sang praises to Mistresses Sophie and Mylissa regarding a recently purchased toy. In some detail she described a piece of equipment which (as most of these things seemed to be) was designed to be locked to the male genetalia. Once in place all one had to do was to pick up a discrete remote control and flick a switch to send an electric jolt to the unit from a distance. She'd tried it out the previous evening on a client while they were out at dinner. Much to the consternation of the other diners, the unfortunate man had spent the evening yelping and squealing in-between gulps of wine and mouthfuls of fine cuisine. Angelique thought it was terrific fun and her colleagues seemed to be of a like mind. Asked for my opinion on such activity I was momentarily flummoxed. Whilst I delved deep for an appropriately sincere response I noticed out of the corner of my eye through the gloom someone was beckoning me with her finger.

I excused myself and made my way over to the individual concerned, a woman I didn't recognise "You're the English spanking guy right?" was her opener. I nodded affirmation. She pursed her ruby red lips, "I got you over here with just one finger. Just think what I could do with all five of them." A courageously blunt conversation opener I must admit. I was about to make a hugely witty response, something along the lines of "I beg your pardon," when Angelique and Sophie arrived to rescue me. She hardly noticed they were there. This statuesque, impossibly proportioned Californian in full leather had a rapaciousness of countenance which re defined the words. I was to discover she was to polite party talk what Pee Wee Herman is to competitive bodybuilding.

There then followed a ruthless interrogation of my private life, which I initially handled by telling her I was a professional bassoonist. This deflected things nicely until I admitted it was a little joke. This was greeted with a baleful stare that nearly had me running for the men's room. She affirmed forcefully she expected me to treat her seriously and she had no time for sexists. I immediately confirmed I believed men and women to be equal to which she responded, "Ah so you're boastful as well are you?" She was serious. She straight out asked me if I was involved with anyone to which I replied thoughtfully, "Yes, myself."

A little later, when I revealed what I actually did for a living she softened her demeanour a mite, no doubt wrongly suspecting that I had deep pockets. I confess I did fan the flames of sarcasm a little when the subject of a recent visit to China came up. "Oh how wonderful," she gushed "Did you see the Pagodas? "See them?" I responded, "I had dinner with them!"

At that moment she left to powder her nose. I turned to my friends remarking, "She's a mite forceful isn't she?" They sniggered and responded that I shouldn't talk about her behind her back but as far as I was concerned it was the only safe way. I also observed that this woman seemed to be undressing me with her eyes. "Impossible," I was informed, "She's not laughing."

Upon her return she bizarrely launched into a long diatribe about the men who had unwisely become part of her life in the past. She talked about her last boyfriend and the lack of honesty in their relationship. I couldn't resist responding by observing I'd had no secrets from my last partner…at least none that she knew about. She hardly heard me. "I'm fed up with being treated like a sex object," she said. Ever the sensitive one I offered, "I don't think of you as a sex object." "You don't have to insult me," she snapped and stormed off. Remember, don't look for logic!

Why is it always those with the least to say generally say the most? I speak from experience of course, being continually guilty of it but you know what I mean. Pascal said *"All the troubles of men and women are caused by one single thing, which is their inability to stay quietly in a room."* In my defence I don't practice what I preach because of course I'm not the kind of person I'm preaching to.

Almost tripping over some guy who was busy doing all sorts of strange things to a seated woman's feet, we sought other amusement. Yes he was middle aged and overweight but at least he wasn't naked. I thanked heaven for small mercies. "Hi Bob," chimed Melissa. He looked up from his chosen mode of entertainment with a sheepish grin. I recognised him from a previous event. I'd evaluated him as the sort of character who, given half a chance, would have grown an unsatisfactory moustache who probably reads biographies about people he's never heard of. I also very strongly suspected he was a man who would choose his own furniture. Understandably we moved quickly on.

Later, much to Mylissa and Angelique's enormous amusement, I indiscreetly related my encounter with 'Goddess Grossly Overweight'. I then cast litigious aspersions on 'Mistress who didn't know the names of her own implements' and gave a colourful account of some of my 'War Stories' since my arrival in the City. In turn they revealed some of their own War Stories', stories so bizarre and hilarious I realised my own anecdotes belonged not in the army but merely in the Peace Corps. Mylissa wobbled off uncertainly on her inordinately high heels to refill her wine glass and a chirpy voice announced the arrival of 'Jenny'. Actually it was Jenny together with that seemingly most widespread of all accessories in the city, a trembling whippet. She picked up the tiny shivering bag of bones, clutched it to her chest, and held forth on her views about such and such a domme. Model car racing club politics once again abounded so I too made for the kitchen to re charge my drink.

Whilst seeking out a suitable beverage amongst those on display Mylissa offhandedly mentioned, as if she were discussing the weather, that her boyfriend was currently locked in a cage at their home. I chuckled at the thought. Later Angelique confirmed this was indeed the case and in fact a regular occurrence. Evidently he loved it. Was this a zoo fetish perhaps? With glass of wine in hand I made to leave but Mylissa was blocking my path. There was an odd look in her eye and she suddenly seemed much taller. She grabbed my chin and said in a voice I almost didn't recognise, "You won't be so upbeat when I've got you on your knees in front of me Englishman," and with that she slapped me round the face. Not brutally but enough for me realise a glass of wine (or seven) too many had been imbibed. At that instant Lady Sophie put her face around the door "Mylissa!" she ordered "Behave!" And with that the moment was gone. We both poured her into a cab and watched her disappear into the night. Oh, and their 'War Stories'? Patience...

The aforementioned Jenny was a well known submissive who was universally liked. A no nonsense kinkster who spent her days as an angel of mercy tending the sick at a hospital and her evenings indulging her almost insatiable fetish needs of which spanking was most certainly one. She gave me a challenging look and said, "These guys say you can dish out the British stuff. Lets see what you've got." Lady Sophie grinned observing, "This ones a challenge." I winked at her and remarked, "Let the games commence."

The partygoers cleared a space and a chair was put in the centre of the room. I knew they were all expecting a show and I knew Jenny was disdainful (in a nice way) thinking she was hard-core. She'd been told about my ad hoc performances but apparently, as I'm not a 'scene person', was unconvinced. Knowing this and knowing my fledgling reputation was on the line I decided to do something unexpected and put this wonderful little upstart in her place. I knew she'd seen and felt it all right up to single tailing so I chose a different tack.

Experienced kinksters know that when doing an intense or prolonged discipline scene it's considered 'polite' and 'safe' to always give your sub a 'warm up' spanking. This gets the blood flowing and close to the surface of the skin which ensures they mark less and the endorphins start pumping before one gets the 'big guns' out. I knew this is what I would be expected to do and it's exactly what I did.

I saw Jenny's eyes glaze over as I put her over my lap thinking, 'Yawn…a warm up…this is going to be a walk in the park.' I knew the people watching would be thinking, 'Lets hope he gets the bloody warm up over and done with so we can get to see the 'real stuff'.'

I didn't even yank down her underwear or jeans much to everyone's dismay. I just started spanking her across her clothed bottom and started to build up the rhythm. And then I carried on…and on…and on….getting harder all the time. As I continued I could see some of the ensemble realised what I was going for. Five minutes in I was whaling this poor girl across her jeans full force with my hand and she was in the awful situation of realizing her reputation as a hard-core player was at risk. She was discovering I could spank far harder than she ever than she ever thought possible. Ten minutes in she was squirming breathlessly as I carried relentlessly on. By now the room was totally quiet. The first tears came at about twelve minutes and by fifteen she was shrieking at the top of her voice whilst sobbing uncontrollably. Shortly afterwards she shouted, "Fuck me…I'M DONE!"

The room was a hushed silence. No one could believe she'd 'safe worded' on a hand spanking through her jeans. I looked up and said, "Right, that's the warm up over. Lets get down to the serious stuff," and the whole ensemble exploded into laughter. Even Jenny grinned. She gasped, "Fucking hell man, I've never ever had a fucking spanking as fucking hard as that." For the more sensitive reader I've significantly cut back on the number of 'fucks' she actually used. She then dropped her jeans and underwear (You can see why I love these parties) and displayed her rear to the guests…it was absolutely crimson.

Shortly afterwards a cell phones trill broke the silence. The recipient of the call answered it and listened gravely to the caller which he revealed was Melissa's boyfriend. His mistress had arrived home and promptly fallen asleep on the sofa, forgetting to release him from his cage. Could someone please come over and let him out?

Nazca Plains

Chapter Thirteen

Paying to Play Redux

Everything appeared to be going well. That being said, life's grim experiences should have taught me if everything seems to be going well, then I've obviously overlooked something. My normally useless antennae was actually working on this occasion but it had served me so badly in the past I chose to ignore its frantic vibrations. The journey to re establish kink as part of my life had been like manhandling a mattress up a spiral staircase but the effort had been worth it. I was convinced I'd got to where I wanted to go and therefore gazed from my lofty peak believing I had total control of my own destiny. Even 'diaper boy' seemed to have given up. In my down time, replete with arcadian anonymity, I flitted gadfly like around Manhattan enjoying my social existence, balancing my vanilla and kink lives with a deft touch and considered precision. I glanced down my nose as lesser mortals went about their lives of bovine drudgery whilst I lauded myself for the once again eclectic nature of my lifestyle.

Thus I made my way to Sutton place for one of my regular rendezvous with Trust Fund Trudy. A woman who was proving to be in possession of more hang ups than the average clothes cabinet; hang-ups which should have indicated caution. Indeed they did, I was just enjoying myself too much to notice them, like the occasion we went to dinner and she'd also unexpectedly invited her parents. This was a shock and as enjoyable as falling downstairs in traction. Instantly on guard (and being British) I'd donned my cloak of humility and took time out to make an inordinate number of suitably self-deprecating comments to impress. I'm now mature enough to know modesty is the art of encouraging people to find out for themselves how wonderful you are. The father had apparently had a full charisma bypass and had his personality surgically removed at birth. The mother was possessed of a voice which would have been better utilized etching crystal than for communication. By the end of dessert I'd discovered old people really are just like ordinary people…but older and less interesting.

In addition to this cringing repast Trudy's quirkiness had slowly revealed itself in a plethora of ways. Investigation confirmed she had a moral compass which would have surprised a zoo animal and a self confessed on going commitment to masturbation which seriously threatened permanent repetitive strain injury. Of the Internets seventeen million spanking pages she'd appeared to have made a serious dent in the objective of reading all of them and her play fantasises had reached a byzantine level of perverse inventiveness. An inventiveness which sometimes had me scratching my head at the level to which she yearned to descend. And then there were the negatives.

There was her propensity to call me at increasingly odd hours with her newest scene ideas, despite being told not to. Additionally I discovered she was a self-harmer. This condition manifest itself by her addiction to American Idol and an inexplicable appreciation of Kenny G. Serious problems indeed.

By now, under my tender ministrations, she'd been spanked, caned, strapped, flogged, tawsed, paddled and hair brushed. She'd also been bound, blindfolded, prodded, poked, pricked and clamped. Indeed Trudy had endured all of the above in seemingly infinite combinations. In turn, at her request, I'd been the wicked uncle, cruel father, strict headmaster, professional disciplinarian, the head monk (which was a right howler) and an abusive intruder. I'd rejected her most recent uncomfortable concoction, the head torturer for a Colombian drug cartel, suggesting my accent wasn't up to it. I'd also declined her request to scour Manhattan for a Nazi Commandants outfit feeling unusually squeamish of crossing the boundaries of good taste. Her relentless enthusiasm notwithstanding, she was beginning to blur the lines between fantasy and reality.

With these weighty thoughts on my mind I mooched down First Avenue on a wet afternoon aware that events 'Trudy wise' were getting out of hand. Something would have to be said. I paused briefly to adjust the collar on my trench coat prior to lowering my head and continued pushing into the rain. As I perambled the slick streets an ominous wind suddenly tore the umbrella from my hand. Above me, dark clouds scudded fitfully across a forbidding sky as if on an urgent mission...do you think I've set the scene well enough?

The nadir occurred as I reached 56th St. My trilling cell phone displayed Trudy's number. I ducked under an awning out of the rain and answered. "Could you pick up some wine on the way over?" she gushed. I heard a mans voice in the background. "Who's that?" I inquired. The normal mellifluousness of her voice vanished and took on a far more urgent tone. "It was supposed to be a surprise," she replied, "It's my new boyfriend Gerry. I want you to show me how to top him."

"Not a surprise I really appreciate Trudy," was my terse response. "I don't 'do' men, unless he wants to fess up for a single tail which I very much doubt." "No silly," she replied, "Nothing like that. I just want you to tie him up and do some cock and ball torture. So's I can see how it's done." At that moment I was the one hoping to be abducted by aliens. Anything to get out of this nightmare. "He's hung like a baby's arm," She added. On the 'unwanted information scale', her last revelation registered around eleven out of ten.

Of course, having some myself, I've nothing against male genetalia but the idea of getting up close and personal with a set that wasn't my own held no appeal whatsoever. Equally I've always been put off by that insensitive bit at the base of the penis...a man. Aghast at her presumption I curtained our association with immediate effect and trudged miserably home. Marcus Aurelius, scribbling away in AD 120 remarked *The object in life is not to be on the side of the majority, but also to escape finding oneself in the ranks of the insane.* Concerning Kink these were very wise words indeed.

I consoled myself that evening by taking up a kind offer of drinks from Mark. He'd taken time out from his demanding schedule of serial colonoscopies without aesthetic to catch up on socialising. When I finally caught up with his screeching posse I could tell, as usual, he was hornier than a Viking Helmet shop. He didn't even notice my arrival for a full ten minutes, concentrating instead on an intense set of tonsil tennis with Steve, a young Asian guy. Unbeknownst to me at the time I was very shortly going to see a lot more of Steve, an awful lot more. After digesting the days strange turn of events I had no inclination things were about to get even more bizarre.

The following days challenges started around noon. Angelique called. "A friends in a bit of a fix and I was hoping you could help her out," she said, "Can I give her your number? Her names Mistress Marcie, sorry I can't chat, I've got to roger someone half to death in ten minutes, byeeee." And with that she was gone. Who was I to refuse?

Things ramped up a bit further when I returned to the apartment from a business meeting. On a recent trip aboard to a far-flung country I was amused to note in the hotel store, next to the toothpaste was, incredibly, an impressive display for 'Delay Spray' for *longer performance.* The accompanying delightfully gaudy literature in appalling English featured a smiling young couple who were evidently well pleased with the product. I secured one thinking it would be an amusing item with which to entertain friends. When I'd returned home some weeks previously I'd totally forgotten all about it. The first thing I do when I return from any trip is to unceremoniously empty my suitcase onto the bedroom floor. Whilst sorting through all the debris I failed to notice my 'spray' was nowhere to be seen.

Today was 'cleaner' day. I strode into my freshly cleaned bedroom and to my abject horror saw the spray sitting neatly on my newly dusted bed side locker. The cleaner had evidently found it in a corner or under the bed and considerately placed it where she though I may need it. How was I going to face her? To mention it, telling her it was merely a gag, may be too obvious, but not to mention it inferred guilt by silence. Whilst chewing my fingernails over this wretched dilemma I received the promised phone call from Angelique's friend, Mistress Marcie. The day started to get weirder.

At the last soiree I'd attended I spent an uncomfortable few minutes trying to end a conversation with short rotund individual with a tan like an old kipper and the intelligence of a pebble. From what I could gather from his touretts driven wittering he made spanking implements and had heard that I regarded myself as a connoisseur of such things. He engaged me with a passionate urgency concerning his skill in such matters whilst sweating like in a pig in ditch and spraying me with liberal doses of dandruff. Evidently he thought of me as a potential new client for his home made offerings and clearly felt that the sheer force of his almost nonexistent personality would persuade me to part with hard cash. I naturally have compassion for anyone with a skin complaint, especially someone who sports a face like the north end of a duck flying south, and so I affected a modest interest in his pitch.

With an iron will I held back from voicing my opinion that he should perhaps move out of his parents basement and perhaps maybe think about putting all that internet time into going to the gym, but, cognisant I was a guest, I demurred. Instead of saying "Do you mind please just going away?" I ordered a tailor made paddle and fled as soon as politesse allowed.

The aforesaid piece de resistance arrived shortly after I'd discovered the delay spray debacle. Upon opening the package I was initially confused as I didn't recall having recently ordered a cheese board. Upon checking the invoice I realised this was the 'paddle'. An implement so thick that if used, wouldn't just knock your contact lenses out, you'd have been risking a detached retina. Glaring at the waste of wood and spitting venom I answered Mistress Marcie's call.

"Hi," she said, "Thanks so much for this. Angelique said you'd help out. My regular guy let me down at the last minute and I'm desperate. My address is...I'll get you up to speed when you arrive." "I'm sorry but…," I stumbled "The address is…," she confirmed, "Is 300 dollars for an hour OK?" "Yes but…," I tried to get a word in. "Wonderful," she breathed. "I need you here in thirty minutes." And with that she hung up. Bemused, I jumped into a cab whilst trying to get Angelique on the phone. After a few attempts I remembered she was currently impaling someone on a piece of stiff rubber and so, a mite curious, I awaited my arrival at the proscribed destination. If she wanted a picture hung then I was up to that. Maybe it was something heavy which needed moving. I certainly wasn't going to take money from a lady for rendering some household assistance.

Like so many Manhattanites, Mistress Marcie had a dog. A real dog though. An amiable Labrador. I was to learn he took great interest in viewing the eclectic proceedings that took place in her apartment. Whenever a victim arrived and was instructed to go into the playroom Buster would solemnly follow and take up a vantage point on the piano stool. There he would watch the various activities through hooded eyes, yawning occasionally if the standard of play didn't meet with his expectations. I liked him immediately, as indeed I did Mistress Marcie. "Busters a connoisseur of kink," she enthused and, hearing his name, he wagged his tail vigorously. Looking at Marcie's trim frame, if I'd have had a tail I'd have wagged it too. She was lovely. I settled for an air kiss and a friendly handshake.

"Righty," I said, rubbing my hands together theatrically "What's the problem?" She then led me into her living room where I was confronted by a nervous looking young man in a dark sombre suit sporting an admirably courageous hat. A full beard and long curling forelocks completed the picture. A Hassidic Jew. The most devout of that race and, in the UK, for reasons best known to themselves, devout drivers of Volvos as well. These were the men whose wives were required to shave their heads and wear wigs. I'd also been informed their mating rituals were fairly unique. Something to do with a hole in a sheet but my ignorance prevents any further possibly speculative disclosures.

Marcie then broke my reverie saying, "Meet our client." I stood speechless. Well, almost speechless. I made to say something but all that escaped my mouth was a thin squeak. I realised I'd inadvertently stepped into the twilight zone. There are some situations in life which not only can one not prepare for, one would bet large sums of money, life savings amounts even, that they would never happen at all. This was such a situation…

Isaac (for that was his name) related he'd always been into spanking but he'd never done it. In order that he followed the tenants of his religion he'd confessed his proclivities and needs to his Rabbi (or whoever the next guy up in the Hassidic management chain was) and asked his advice. Incredibly the old man had said "Ah, yes. A common problem. Here's what you do my son. There are women called Dominatrices. They can see to your needs. However, in order to receive my blessing and for this to be correct in the eyes of God they mustn't actually touch you with their hands. Furthermore there must be a man present and he too must help with your punishment."

Looking at my astonishment Marcie laughed. "Don't worry," she said, "There's no over the knee stuff." And this made it alright? Even if there really is a venerable white haired omnipresent being in the sky who controls our destinies I couldn't imagine him sanctioning this, unless he had more of a sense of humour than I'd previously been led to believe. Back down here on planet Earth I had a different perspective. "It'll be fun," Marcie assured me.

I'm sure by now it's no revelation to state that topping a male Hassidic Jew for hard cash had never been high on my list of 'must do's. Whilst probably not the worst job in the world (that, obviously, being a pole cleaner at a strip club) it certainly wasn't how I would choose to pay the rent. I silently cursed the eight-year-old Susan who'd set me on this long and fraught road to perdition. Of course I was letting myself off way too easily. I was overlooking my own blight ridden, intellectually lightweight, morally bankrupt excuse for a personality. But, hey, a friend in need right? And three hundred dollars is three hundred dollars. I'd decided I'd accept the cash. It would have simply been bad manners not to. I suddenly regretted not bringing my new cheeseboard along.

So, I'd crossed the line. I'd topped professionally. I'd even got a tip. I was a male 'pro domme'. Visions of beautiful women paying me to thrash them on a regular basis raced briefly through my mind. There was cash to be had from my hobby. The day had been most strange and it was about to get even stranger. Someone named Steve called me. "I'm sorry," I said, "I don't know any Steves." Further inquiry revealed him to be Marks Asian tonsil tennis partner. "Mark gave me your number," he explained, "I told him I wanted to talk to you about golfing lessons." "I don't give golfing lessons," I replied patiently. "I know," he said, "But I do." "Sorry," I replied," I don't want any." "That wasn't really why I wanted your number," he confessed. I once again stepped into bizzarro world. "I heard about what you did at the club. I was wondering if you'd beat me."

Now, being a fully-fledged professional, I didn't miss a beat "It's five hundred Dollars an hour," I snapped, "And there's no 'over the knee' or any funny stuff." In fairness to him he didn't miss a beat either "Fine," he replied. Well, he wasn't a beautiful woman but, hey, it was a start!

My unusual day ended with a quaking naked Asian man in my lounge. Something I certainly hadn't anticipated when I got up that morning or indeed any morning. As he disrobed I was reminded of some words once spoken by Domme Jackeline, "Oh, it's such a joy when they're in shape." Never a truer work spoken. Steve was in wonderful shape, a fact which met with my total approval. He'd arrived on time, handed me over the cash and stripped as I demanded. As he stood nervously awaiting his retribution I told him I expected some self-control and stoicness. You could have cut the atmosphere with a knife. Unable to stop myself I continued "I want it as quiet as a narcoleptics anonymous meeting in here." He exploded into uncontrollable giggles. So did I. Not for long though. The clock was ticking and business is business.

Sixty-three minutes later a suitably chastened and florid faced Steve bade me farewell and was out of the door like a gay son in a Mormon household. Now a total of eight hundred dollars richer as a result of my activities (plus tip), I reflected that whilst the day had been bizarre, it had also most definitely been profitable. A text broke my chain of thought revealing a beseeching note from Trudy begging me to resume activities. On a roll I replied, 'Three hundred and fifty dollars an hour, six hundred for two, no communication between visits except to book an appointment'. Thirty seconds later I received a reply. "OK," it said. It seemed I was currently more popular than Justin Bieber at an under fifteens party. Total madness. I wasn't just immersed in kink, I was drowning in it! Pay to play suddenly meant something very different.

Desperately seeking to regain the balance I mistakenly thought I'd already achieved I waded back into my vanilla existence. The following evening saw me escorting a young lady to the culinary delights of fashionable eatery which nestled comfortably a few blocks east of my humble abode. It's an elegant establishment where a practiced raised eyebrow brings servile waiters scuttling to ones table in short order. As befits my worldly persona I was beguilingly charming, sensitive and courageously witty. She was not I regret to say. The woman concerned was not my type, i.e. she didn't jump into bed with me at the first opportunity, explaining she really preferred 'Jocks'. My revelation that I was half Scots was apparently insufficient to persuade her I could deliver.

Undeterred I pressed forward shortly afterwards with a thirty six year old divorced nurse. Nurses are normally good fun because they've seen so much and take no bullshit, so at worst I was hoping for an engaging encounter. It's been said that 'One swallow does not a summer make' but, lets face it, it can certainly help make an evening.

A French restaurant specialising in food from Provence was my choice of meeting place. I had high hopes of fine wines, sparkling company and an ambiance which reflected the romance of The Carargue. I felt like relaxing into the rich nose of a fine Vacqueyras or maybe even a Bandol. We could perhaps enjoy an evening pleasantly accompanied by the aroma of fine Périgord truffle.

Once again I was the perfect companion. I managed to suppress my normal sympathetic apathy and stun my companion with acerbic and keenly observed opinions on life in general. This was my opening gambit. I then followed this with my 'meaningful' bit; apparently hesitatingly exposing the depths of my humanity in a way that would have made Ghandi feel uncomfortable. I finished off my performance with a deluge of sparkling anecdotes which would not have been out of place at Nobel Prize reception. A truly Oscar winning performance. And the result? God, multi orgasmic women are such a sweat. One part of you feels great for the service you're providing and the other part of you just gets exhausted. Not that this formed any part of my nocturnal activities because I'm far too circumspect to bore you with tales of my awesome performance. I'm bluffing of course. My technique consists of frantic and unsophisticated fumbling around my partners nether regions in the hope I touch something that works, but, occasionally, I get lucky.

I walked home in love with New York. I thought emotionally and with true affection of the city that never sleeps. The music of Gershwin, skating on the ice in Central Park, the Yankees... the sigh of midnight trains in empty stations, Opps, what am I waffling on about? OK OK, I'll get back to the kink. Kink in the Hamptons actually. Yes it exists. Well, it does now anyway.

Being a product of the British lower middle classes, as I grew up the concept of having more money than God was somewhat abstract. The delineations between old money and new money was also irrelevant as I was normally focussed on the concept of 'no money'. My first real understanding of privilege was falling in with a crowd of Toffs on a wretched Boy Scout Jamboree camp. I listened in wonder as these Etonian (or Harrovian) twats talked in a language I barely understood. The only two things I learned that weekend were that they were regularly beaten at school and that they all enjoyed a good session of 'circle jerk'. I'd never heard of the expression and, after having it explained to me, I wanted to hear about it no more. I only knew I could never regard a chocolate biscuit (cookie) in the same way again. And that's all I'm saying. I ended the weekend with a serious sense of low esteem and a realisation that being poor was a drawback bigger than an elephant's foreskin.

I mention this as suddenly privilege was in the air. I was dining at The Harvard Club prior to jumping on the Hampton Jitney for a full evenings nonsense which was to put eighteen hundred dollars (plus expenses) in my back pocket. Trust Fund Trudy was funding the session (including travelling time and an overnight stay) having twice previously paid for my services with no fuss or complaint (or annoying phone calls). Kink fuelled by inexhaustible cash is always a fun combination. The Harvard club, as its name suggests, is an elite establishment on 5th Avenue. Evidently having actually been to Harvard is not enough to get a membership. One has to be forwarded, seconded (and probably thirded and fourthed) to even get an interview. Unreal!

Scowling portraits of former members glowered down at me whilst I concentred on not making any social faux pas and addressed the frankly inadequate cuisine. Unfazed by the embarrassingly august mock pedigree of this fascist enclave, I wondered what the other club members would have thought if they'd known they were entertaining a part time male dominatrix. Whilst they waffled on about golf I realised Trudy and I wouldn't be the only ones dressing up in ridiculous clothes that weekend. I mean, have you seen what a serious golfer regards as suitable attire? I once read Golf is the only game where grown men walk around looking like they've been dressed by their mothers. I'd also read that a golf course is the only place you'll see white men dress like black pimps. A bit of leather seems pretty tame in comparison...and a lot more enjoyable.

My excessively corpulent dining companion enquired as to my weekend plans as he tucked into his extravagantly generous portion of key lime pie. "The Hamptons," I offered, "No golf but I will be beating my servants savagely with something close to a golf club. Does that count?" The ensuing guffaw saw him eject the dessert from his mouth with some ferocity. A waiter was there in a heartbeat to clear things up. It set me thinking about such matters. I've always believed waiters should be like barmen. After all, if you're drunk in bar and you ask for more alcohol the barman can say, "Actually sir, I think you've had enough," and refuse to serve you. Surely waiters should do the same with fat people who order desserts? Just sayin' is all.

The reason for my dining companions excessive laughter was due to the fact that he too was a fervent kinkster. I'd met him at one of the gatherings and found him to be a tirelessly amusing raconteur with a rich and eclectic sense of humour. We'd swapped patently untrue stories about tattooists with epilepsy, blind body piercers, dwarf chiropractors and speculated on the commercial possibilities for Braille copies of *Playboy*. We also found ourselves firmly in agreement on a wide variety of subjects. These ranged from acknowledging the sad fact that penis reduction surgery was ridiculously hard to come by to the revelation that truly committed nudists are always the very people you don't want to see naked. Hey, com'on, you know it's true...

Despite the fact he was the sort of man who wears sandals with socks we became firm friends He wasn't actually wearing sandals with socks you understand and I've never seen him do so but I just know he's the sort of guy who would. He was also a serious medical fetishist. He liked nothing better than to be catheterised, have his arms put into casts and be pushed around the city in a wheelchair on a Sunday afternoon by a pretty nurse and good for him. He also on occasion had a penchant for having inordinately large amounts of weights hung from his scrotum. I may not have understood it but I totally approved of his commitment.

It turned out to be a totally outrageous lie that Trudy's boyfriend was hung like a baby's arm. Gerry was equipped like a fucking Brontosaurus. I'd never seen or even heard of anything quite like it. He could have been a champion pole-vaulter without having to invest any money whatsoever on the necessary equipment. Though I'd resolved to go nowhere near the damn thing its size made it difficult to avoid if you were in the same room. I was only grateful it wasn't actually in motion as it could have taken someone's eye out. The reason for its relatively stationary position was due the fact that at that moment he was restrained naked on a bed with straps applied by Trudy under my instruction.

Gerry had had quite a time of it over the previous couple of hours being subject to his girlfriend's fervent interest in extracting as much out of the session as she possibly could. He'd had to watch apparently poker faced as I stripped her front of him and made her assume all manner of humiliating positions whilst beating her to tears. I say apparently poker faced as his visage was obscured by a leather hood kindly supplied by Trudy. At one point he looked to be about to try and intervene but being restrained to a sturdy chair at the time made it difficult. A ball gag didn't help either. He'd squirmed and grunted unattractively whilst I bound her up and attached a variety of colourful clothes pins about her trim physique. I was about to start working her over with a pinwheel when his contortions became even more pronounced and urgent. Ever the compassionate one I briefly removed his gag. "Thank Christ," he breathed, "I gotta use the bathroom...like right now!"

A serious note on safety here for the curious or the newbie. Obviously if someone's gagged they can't use a safe word to stop matters. The way round this is to agree a hand signal and for the top to regularly check the victims hands for such a signal. Gerry's signal was to do the bird...a fact he'd totally forgotten. You'll correctly surmise from this that it's best to play with someone who's packing a full compliment of brain cells. Gerry, whilst amiable, was a mite deficient in this area;

the majority of his physical development had seemingly taken place between his legs and not his ears. Nonetheless he was certainly game. I think prior to encountering Trudy the kinkiest thing he'd ever done was have sex with the lights on. Until recently, as far as he was concerned, Miss Whiplash was a woman suffering from neck trouble after a car accident. He'd had to endure a lot since meeting her. Mind you, looking at the size of his penis, so had she.

I'd arrived in the Hamptons with my bag of tricks some hours earlier (I'll not say which Hampton to save any potential blushes) and my first reaction upon alighting from the Jitney was that the sidewalks were cleaner than my crockery and probably a lot more healthy to eat off. My next observation was a church with valet parking (yes really) and a main street which had an ambiance I'd not seen since viewing 'The Stepford Wives'. I jumped into quite the most immaculate taxicab I'd ever seen and made for Trudy's beach club were we'd arranged to meet. Upon arrival at the appointed destination I noted the Beach club was on the left hand side of the road and the clubs car park directly opposite offering, incredibly, valet parking for those too physically challenged to walk fifty feet. This seemed to be everyone.

Upon walking into the club the first thing that confronted me was a prominent notice board bearing the legend 'The Following Members Have Not Paid Their Dues'. Charming I'm sure. Next to this embarrassing sign was a small shop. Endeavouring to get into the sprit of things I looked through their t-shirts featuring the name of the place whilst wincing at some of the prices. "What's the cheapest shirt in the shop?" I enquired brightly. "You're wearing it," was the tart reply. Blinking back tears of meanness I eventually forked over the required cash for a purchase.

After having been cleared for entry by a 'security guy' with a brain the size of a dried pea I found myself walking through Penny Loafer and top sider heaven to the bar. I was dazzled by an onslaught of pastel shades and New England chique. As I ducked through and around the plethora of white tennis visors I was aware the cognoscente of the establishment appeared to be either very old, and I mean absolutely bloody ancient or young and perfect...and I do mean perfect. These people looked like they'd been created on a 'perfect people' production line. Perfect white teeth flashed from perfect faces atop perfect bodies. I sucked in my stomach, clamped my lips over my 'English' teeth and slunk to where I saw Trudy with her new beau.

"Hi," she gushed, "We're going to have a few drinks here before we go back and start. We want to make sure all the servants have gone for the day." It was the inclusion of the word 'all' in her statement that made me realise that I was definitely fiscally challenged. That having been said she discreetly slipped me an envelope stuffed with a wad of cash which made me feel slightly better. "This is Gerry," she offered. And indeed so it was. Gerry was a man of few words and of those few words only a very small number ever proved to be of interest but, as I said, at least he was game. Some polite questioning revealed he was something in local government, probably a piece of office equipment I surmised. With the way he weakly acquiesced to Trudy's every demand I suspected it was a rubber stamp, or was it a doormat? A little later, after offering muted appreciation of our environment, I related I had once been cautioned in a gentleman's country club in the UK for playing croquet without a jacket. Trudy sniggered, Gerry thought I was being serious. The funny thing is...I was!

We left in the early evening for the short journey back to her palatial retreat. My entire apartment would have fitted into her garage. This is not an exaggeration. As we walked to the house I paused for a moment to enjoy the sunset. It was the sort of sunset which made me think to myself how insignificant I was. Then I remembered that I felt that way every most of the time so I cheered myself up with the thought of what was too come, at least the bits with Trudy anyway.

Some time later I watched with some amusement as Trudy, following my directions, went through the various implements on Gerry's virgin butt. He sucked it up admirably with barely a sound. He didn't react the same way with cock and ball torture though. Strapped naked and spread-eagled to the bed his girlfriend, with squeals of delight, tied, twisted, tweaked, pinched, pricked and squeezed as I offered enthusiastic instruction from a safe distance. Gerry wasn't squealing… he was yelling. He was discovering what it was really like in 'Trudy World'. Having finished demolishing his wedding tackle she moved onto his nipples. I winced as she set about them as if she was aggressively tuning a radio.

When the session was over our hostess was flushed with excitement whereas Gerry was merely flushed. Demolishing the better part of a bottle of wine in under ten minutes he made his excuses and took an early night. As he wobbled his way bow legged across the room nursing his swollen reproductive equipment I almost felt sorry for him. It was probably the first time in his life he'd regretted possessing such a generous endowment.

Trudy and I retired to her back yard. Well that's what she called it. I'd have used the description 'a vast rolling estate'. It's said that money talks but wealth whispers. It was whispering so quietly now I could hardly make out what it was saying. We sipped wine by a beautiful water feature groaning with Koi carp. I indicated my approval of the fabulous creatures. She launched into an enthusiastic exhortation of the calmness she felt they gave her. Ever seeking to educate I murmured, "Did you know the Japanese call them *Shiramugi*? It means white. They call them that because the first specimens that came from the Caspian Sea were a perfect pearl white in colour. It was the Japanese who somehow bred colour into them. The really brightly coloured ones are called *Kokugyo* which means 'living jewel'." I then smugly sipped my wine in the knowledge my stock would have gone up a few points and maybe also my hourly rate. Evidently those few points were the straw that broke the camels back. She went quiet and grabbed my hand saying, "You say such wonderful things. Can you stay tomorrow and do it all again? I've got plenty of cash in the house."

Damn, I was getting good.

Chapter Fourteen

War Stories

"This," announced Angelique, "Is Mistress Daphne." I was eventually meeting the final star in the very modestly sized constellation that comprised the elite of New York's kink firmament. Mistress Angelique, Mistress Daphne, Lady Sophie, Domme Mylissa and Mistress Marcie were at the very top of Mount Everest. Domme Jackeline was also on a pinnacle but, by her own choice, she occupied a totally different mountain, a mountain which she resolutely owned and a peak that despite its equally lofty height was very much under the radar. Yes I know that sentence doesn't quite make sense but I'm sure you know what I mean. I very much respected all of them and their individual choices. I also liked them enormously; their wickedly pragmatic countenances, unselfishness and generosity of spirit having helped me pave my way back to that which I'd missed so much.

Daphne's sardonic smile won me over well before her motivational physique hit me like a runaway truck. Adorned in a ubiquitous pencil skirt and a de rigueur white blouse she defined the role of governess. A perfect outfit for the session I was about to conduct. A demonstration of English Discipline with Chloe. The Chloe who was currently staring at Daphne with open-mouthed appreciation. I gave her a sideways grin "Steady," I urged and we all laughed. Chloe was looking forward to this in the same way that Juiced Jeanine had almost been looking forward to meeting Domme Jackeline. This was despite the fact I'd reminded her of the time honoured expression, "Don't wish too hard…"

You'll recall at our first encounter Jeanine had bemoaned the fact she'd never been dealt with by a 'truly cruel woman'. Despite her brief alcoholic escapade she'd subsequently proved to be an intelligent and lively player and we'd become firm friends. At one of our encounters I'd briefly alluded to one of my sessions with Jackeline and she'd seized upon it like a desert locked man encountering a jug of iced water. I nimbly defected a barrage of questions stating simply. "She's real, extremely private and absolutely not for the faint hearted." This was like a red rag to a bull to Jeanine as I knew it would be and so, on her next trip to NYC, at her request I'd made the arrangements. I'd telephoned Jackeline saying. "Jeanine's a genuine enthusiast but she's got a bit of an attitude." There was a brief silence "She won't try that with me I assure you," she snapped. With a wry smile I called the object of our conversation and told her it was 'on'.

On the appointed evening the breathless and excited recipient arrived at my apartment in a heightened state. She was clearly nervous but trying her very best not to show it and as a result she was enjoying herself hugely. Her mixture of fear and anticipation was palpable and she covered up by making small comments laced with unconvincing bravado. I'd honed her senses even further the evening beforehand by sadistically calling her saying. "Look, you don't have to do this to prove anything. I can easily cancel this now and I won't think anything less of you. This woman is very severe and she'll go all the way. I'm not really sure you're ready for it." There was a silence. "It's OK," I said gently, "I'll cancel it." "No no no," she blustered, "I'm ready, really I am," as I knew she would. She was almost pleading bless her. Now though, the hour was nearly at hand and she was like a cat on a hot tin roof. I'd never seen her like this. When my doorbell went she literally leapt up off her chair. "Face the other way and put your hands on your head," I told her. And with that I let Domme Jackeline in.

She ducked into the bathroom to change while Jeanine quaked with her nose pressed against the wall. The apartment was a quiet as a complaints department in a parachute factory. A click of a lock heralded Jackelines exit from the bathroom and she walked into the lounge resplendent once again in her body hugging once piece black dress, stockinged legs, high heels and immaculate brunette bob. "Turn around Jeannine," she said quietly and her victim complied. Her face was a picture. Stark terror. Her face also reflected something else equally interesting. Jeannine was a rabid heterosexual but upon seeing Jackeline she'd instantly fallen in lust, a fact she shamefacedly confirmed later.

Suddenly to Jackeline and I's confusion Jeannine was fumbling in her bag. She withdrew a beautifully wrapped small box and offered it up. "Chocolates," she stammered, "I thought you might like them." This was not the Jeanine I knew. Mind you I wasn't the 'me' I knew when I was submitting to this woman either. A hint of a smile passed the dominatrices lips, "Thank you," she breathed, taking the gift and depositing it gently on the bed. "Now," she continued, "I want you to get on your hands and knees and symbolically kiss each of my shoes." A look of horror flashed across Jeannine's face. "Now," snapped Jackeline, "Don't keep me waiting." In a heartbeat this proud non-submissive Amazonian meekly complied. Perfect. "Very well," she continued, "Fetch me the dragon cane." There were apparently going to be no warm up spankings this evening.

A moment or so later Jeanine was bent over the side of my sofa bereft of her skirt and underwear. Cane in hand Jackeline bent over her victim and spoke softly. "We'll start with a hundred I think. I want you to count and thank me for every stroke. Do I make myself absolutely clear?" Jeanine nodded rapidly, "I can't hear you," prompted her tormentor. "Yes Mistress," she stammered. With that her chastiser stood up, raised the cane theatrically and brought it down with a resounding crack over her supplicants rear. A livid red tramline appeared and Jeannine gasped. A moment later she said it. "One Mistress, thank you Mistress." And so it went on…for a hundred strokes. Magnificent. A word which applies to both players.

Once again, a non-kinkster won't understand this comment but the true kinkster will. This was totally beautiful to watch. Jeannine needed everything she had to endure her chastisement. Every part of her body language and exhalation of breath demonstrated this. Whilst you could see her struggling you could also feel her determination, her determination to get through this and not to disappoint her cool dispassionate mistress. Equally, Jackeline understood this and used her skill to challenge her charge, knowing exactly when to back off and exactly when to push, in essence easing her through the ordeal by the varying of cadence and severity. She was to the cane what Angelique was to the single tail. Its total mistress. It was a privilege to watch.

When the caning was over Jeanine didn't even know what day of the week it was. Jackeline went through various different straps and finished with a light paddle having given Jeanine exactly what she said she wanted. The experience of being dealt with by a genuine sadist. A sadist she may have been but she was an artiste also. As always there wasn't a single low or high blow and not a wrap in sight. As Jeanine was heard to bluster afterwards. "God, that woman's got skill sets up the ying yang." I'm sure this was a compliment.

Upon revealing that the ordeal was over her charge stood up with a flushed face, a sheepish grin and a bottom which would have defrosted a sixteen ounce steak in a block of ice. She thanked Jackeline profusely, thanks that she received with a modest smile. This modest smile was rapidly followed by a wicked grin. She turned to me "Right," she commanded, "It's your turn now. Strip." "What?" I squealed, "We never talked about this?" "Don't make me tell you a second time," she chided. "Do it!" Jeanine couldn't believe what she was hearing. I couldn't believe what I was hearing either! Her face broke into a broad grin as I miserably removed my clothes and bent over the side of the sofa as ordered. A breathtakingly rapid fifty stroke caning followed after which she supplemented with the most brutal paddling I've ever received, pushing me the closest I've ever been to calling off a scene. I couldn't though; I didn't want to disappoint my tormenter. The marks lasted for almost six months.

Within five minutes of finishing, our chastiser was off into the night. I'd originally envisaged her leaving and my talking with Jeanine as she lay on her stomach trying to process what had just happened to her. The reality was she left both of us lying on our stomachs trying to process what had just happened to both of us. God the woman was a bitch and we loved it.

An unexpected benefit to my unplanned thrashing was I could legitimately cancel an enforced visit to the Opera the following evening. The reason being that I literally found it difficult to sit down. I silently thanked my chastiser as I lay on my stomach at home in front of the TV. Somewhere in Manhattan my friends were subjecting themselves to an overweight woman with a large facial mole shrieking in Italian and they were bloody welcome to it. I confess I'm speculating about the mole.

Whilst I set myself up in Angelique's studio for the demo Chloe wandered around the magnificent play space clearly impressed by the quality of what see was seeing. I could only agree. She had appointed it with thought and genuine talent and invested a fortune. A tailor made full suspension rig, the inevitable cage, a plethora of complex leather restraint gear, full body bags, hoods, scary medical equipment, an autoclave for sterilisation (for toys, not the clients) and a selection of corporal implements to tease the most jaded palate. Commitment indeed. Angelique and Daphne chatted whilst opening wine and I caught a bit of the conversation "Anyway," said Angelique, "So I called up Ed and asked if he wanted to come over. You know Ed don't you?" Daphne nodded. "It was great," she continued. "I put him in suspension, catheterised him and sewed his lips together." Daphne nodded attentively and didn't bat an eyelid. My eyelids were batting like crazy. Amongst the wild things this pair were clearly two of the wildest.

I'd met Ed a number of times previously. His almost cherubic African American features constantly sporting a lopsided grin. A highly intelligent and very successful guy to whom kink was not merely very important, it was as necessary as oxygen. His experience of the unusual made my own encounters look like a toddler in a Masonic lodge. His personal range of toys and accoutrements was approaching Angelique's collection and where kink was concerned he wouldn't just rush in where angels fear to tread...he'd ride in naked, flat out on a motor bike without a helmet, through a plate glass window.

Some years previously he discovered a Czech based coven of dominatrices living in a converted castle type affair who ran the whole place as a female supremacy gig. Evidently male slaves (who apparently queued up to get into this place) were expected to have the crap beaten out of them on a regular basis and were made to sleep naked on straw in the stables at night. This bunch of crazed Amazonians were also renowned for their intensely hard core videos and had announced they were seeking men to fess up to their abuse on film. Despite speaking no Czech, Ed was on the next plane. He was not only intelligent, he was bloody brave! Subsequent conversation revealed his lip stitching was a walk in the park compared to what he'd endured over there...

"So I stuck needles through his penis," Daphne was just finishing off a conversation concerning a recent client. I took a deep breath and silently blessed the good Lord for restricting my area of interests. "Ladies," I said, "We're ready to start." Daphne and Angelique sat primly on chairs opposite me and I bade Chloe over my lap. I was nervous. After all I was demonstrating my skills in front of two of the biggest names in the business. I needn't have worried. I whipped down Chloe's jeans and started whaling away. Incredibly I got an audible intake of breath from my audience. Chloe and I had played so much I knew what her limits where and what she liked. Clearly Angelique and Daphne were expecting that I treat this sylph like creature more gently not knowing how hard-core she was.

For almost half an hour I worked on her, swapping positions and implements and finished with the inevitable caning. Chloe stood up with a grin and Daphne enthused "I really enjoyed that, especially the caning." "Would you care to experience it?" I offered. She hesitated for a moment "OK," she agreed, "Just one." With that she stood, walked over to the chair and bent over presenting a most delightful rear end. I took aim and gave her a firm stroke. Angelique winced slightly but Daphne didn't t make a sound. She stood up slowly "MMM," she murmured. She made to turn around then stopped and repositioned herself. "I'll take another five," she grinned. We all laughed. She took five belters.

Prior to this Angelique had thought of domestic discipline as being more about role-play and less about intensity. Now she knew differently. Daphne was far more discipline oriented. This was demonstrated by her taking the cane from my hand and beckoning Chiloe over "Come here little girl," she ordered looking the absolute perfect representation of an English governess. Chloe, still flushed from her session complied with total enthusiasm and bore another twenty-four strokes with admirable fortitude. The evening was turning out very nicely. "My turn," piped up Angelique. "I warn you," she continued, "I top from the bottom like a motherfucker." An interesting turn of phrase and a totally accurate statement. I gave her a hand spanking during which she cursed, cussed and swore vehemently. She did the same for her twelve stroke caning, complaining, moaning and whining about stroke placement, intensity and the position I'd demanded she assume. Bringing matters to a close I had her lying across a chair. I picked up a paddle. "Right," I said, "I can give you five fast ones or ten slow ones." "Fuck you," was the forthright response, so I gave her twelve rapid strokes which finished with her blubbing like a schoolgirl. Much to our enormous amusement she laughingly confessed through her tears, "That wasn't much fun at all. I don't know why I asked."

Over dinner that evening I was as ever struck by the incongruity of looking at our happy smiling little bunch and what the other diners would have thought if they'd know what we'd been up to a mere thirty minutes beforehand. Daphne was enthusing over a recent working trip to London. She was delighted someone had recognised her in the street and even more delighted that the dungeon she worked from had a cell...with a real hose. This was source of great pleasure during some really intense prison scenes. She spoke so enthusiastically it was hard not to be happy for her. She'd arrived back in the US 'totally kinked out' which, knowing Daphne as I came to, must have meant a very great deal of kink indeed and a well deserved bulging purse.

Both Angelique and Daphne and their close colleagues involved themselves in monster scenes, sometimes lasting literally days at a time. Knowing what they charged their clients these men must have had very deep pockets indeed. These scenarios often featured multiple dommes and required a precision in planning which beggars the imagination. These deep-pocketed clients were understandably demanding, having paid a lot of money to scratch their itch. The fact they came back time and again indicates the quality these inventive and highly intelligent women provided. I sat back and soaked up some of their more amusing stories, a few of which demand to be repeated.

The combination of confectionary and kink is at first glace an unlikely marriage. Combine such a scenario with black plastic trashcan liners and a chubby accountant called Bob and you've got an even less likely fusion. Bob however was wealthy and correctly identified it as a well paying job for todays modern diverse dominatrix. Deriving enjoyment from having cakes and assorted pastries thrown at you is not the most usual of persuasions but it's nonetheless a well-documented activity, documented by whom though I cannot begin to imagine. For the committed accountant this was a merely 'entry level'.

The armchair psychoanalysts amongst you are probably already beginning to stroke your metaphorical beards in an attempt to speculate on the origin of this gentlemen's itch. Don't bother. You'll simply end up with a headache. And Bob didn't like having cakes thrown at him. He liked to throw them himself, his preferred target being an attractive woman dressed up in…black plastic bin liners. The terms 'cakes' was far too generic for our protagonist. He had standards and rigid requirements. They specifically had to be gateaux of the lightest constitution stuffed with copious quantities of fresh cream. This culinary elitism was probably a good thing for the Dominatrix concerned. The thought of being caught a smart blow across the head by an enthusiastically flung two day old English fruitcake is not an appealing one.

And why was this a job for a dominatrix anyway? Well, apart from the fact that he offered an obscene amount of money for the service, he then demanded to be resoundingly beaten with cake mixing spatula whilst clearing up the mess afterwards. I'd have personally used a rolling pin.

If Bob had a cake fetish then Piers had a rampaging opera glove obsession which took the concept of preoccupation to almost celestial levels. Unlike the confection loving book keeper there was no mystery behind the origin of Piers proclivities. His dear mother was unwittingly to blame.

A product of the British Upper Classes, membership of which on its own virtually guarantees an alternative sexuality, a six year old Piers had been awoken one night by his mother pulling his dishevelled sheets up to ensure the poor lad didn't catch cold. In doing so she accidently briefly brushed his penis through his pyjamas. Not a dramatic event in itself and surely not an unusual experience for our young hero. The difference this time being that his mother had just returned from the Opera and was wearing the requisite gloves for such an occasion. The moment had changed him dramatically and irrevocably.

She had tucked in his sheets tightly to ensure they stayed in place. The result being that the combination of light restraint and opera gloves was forever linked to the brief instant of pleasure he'd received having his organ touched. He'd never looked back and opera glove makers everywhere had rejoiced and subsequently prospered. He owned thousands of them... literally. His ability to achieve an erection was inextricably linked to the proximity of such an item and more so if combined with tight bed sheets. This was no doubt a source of both curiosity and valued revenue to his local dry cleaner.

Once a month one of Daphne's British colleagues would hear the tell tale THUMP THUMP THUMP as a wheezing Piers dragged one of his numerous epic sized trunks of gloves up three flights of stairs to the apartment where she conducted her business. The man was a good client and Daphne's associate was not without compassion. Accordingly, on his fourth visit she offered him the opportunity of leaving the trunk there for future assignations. He looked at her aghast. "I couldn't do that," he said, "They're my babies." Quite a statement from a high-ranking military officer. After he'd caught his breath the next hour or so would comprise of Daphne's friend tucking and untucking her client in bed whist wearing different Opera gloves...and that was that. Almost.

Piers paid her substantial fee without rancour. He also generously offered her a bonus after the first time they'd played. In an hour she'd managed to get a certain number of opera gloves on and off and replaced with a different variety and then tucked him in X number of times. Piers, with well-practiced military precision, had counted exactly how many gloves she used. He then offered to pay her more if she could up the pace. The result being the lady concerned became a speed glove-removing expert of laudable calibre. She even used to practice between visits. The really ironic thing about

Piers is he actually hated Opera! That much I certainly liked about him.

Humphrey was probably ambivalent about opera gloves but he did like horse racing, bulldogs, shooting small furry animals and striding ruddy faced around his vast country estate bellowing at his staff. You may correctly conclude he was also a member of the British ruling classes. A fish out of water, he stayed in New York for tax reasons for a memorable twelve-month period during which time he (quite correctly) bemoaned the lack of a decent cup of tea, beer that actually has some taste and cricket. He was on his own though as far as the Cricket was concerned. Oh, and Humphrey liked balloons. No, I mean he really liked them, he really liked them an awful lot. He didn't collect the objects of his affection (or was it affliction?) like Piers but he did buy them on an unhealthily regular basis. The origins of his fetish are obscure at best but had something to do with 'nanny' and being naughty at a children's birthday party many years ago. He was naturally into being beaten of course as are the majority of the British aristocracy but unless there was a balloon present to stroke (or preferably a whole bunch of them) the session wouldn't be viewed as satisfactory.

Humphrey's eventual epiphany came one day when a friend persuaded him to join a gym in the city. There for the first time he encountered the large gym balls which are now a feature of all workout establishments. He'd stood mesmerised looking at the three-foot wide monster and realised all his Christmases had come at once. By the end of the day he owned a bright blue example. Thereinafter he solemnly rolled it to all his pre-arranged thrashings, evidencing a barely concealed delight as he bent over it to await his comeuppance. To my knowledge it never burst and I'm told soapy water kept it clean. Nuff said!

One of Stacy's more serious aficionados, who we'll call Gervaise (although his real name was Robert), was a connoisseur of intense cock and ball torture. And when I say connoisseur I mean a hard wired, died in the wool rampaging fanatic. He didn't blame his mother for this, but he did blame a childhood friend who inadvertently set him along this path. Whilst play wresting with an attractive young girl she'd accidently kneed him in crotch. No matter what age you are this is going to be an eye waterer. He was nine at the time. Seeing his evident discomfort the mortified girl had gently soothed him whilst he writhed around on the ground. "It was the soothing that got me," he confessed. Thereinafter started a pattern. If he squeezed his genitals he'd automatically think of a soothing female voice. The greater the pain the greater the soothing and the more aroused he became.

Inevitably, over the years, experimentation followed, though that activity was not without its own inherent dangers. On one occasion his mother caught him tugging vigorously on his scrotum with a pair of pliers whilst reading a girlie magazine. A difficult one to talk your way our of but not as difficult as the time he'd come a hairs breadth from having to explain why he was squeezing his penis in his fathers vice. Apparently it was a very close call. Nonetheless, despite the occasional cringing drawback he persisted. For Gervaise genital pain was pleasure and that was what led him to my ex landlady's door.

Stacy was no slouch in the dishing out pain department and she'd set about him with a gusto, commencing with a no holes barred kick to the balls. His knees had weakened slightly but he made not a murmur. Evidently she'd then cracked her knuckles, fixed her face with a determined look and unleashed all sorts of hell on his equipment short of actually tearing it off. He not only endured stoically, he'd also endured silently. Relishing a challenge she'd bade me accompany her to the hardware store to supplement the available devices she had for the task in hand. I suggested a hammer combined with a cheese grater. She giggled and told me to grow up. It never happened.

Her ingenuity surprises me even now when I think about it. She finally got his mark. Gentlemen readers may wish to cross their legs at this point. She purchased some industrial strength sandpaper and then glued this to the inside of a used up toilet roll. She then liberally sprinkled the interior with Tabasco Sauce. I'll leave the rest to your imagination. She had a client for life. At the time Gervais was childless and I strongly suspect he still is. I was also going to tell you about her other unusual client, 'Billy the button fetish boy' but I rather think his name tells you all you need to know.

Unlike the aforementioned enthusiasts Tarquin (yes really) was truly kinky. A serious fetishist. Not for him the mainstream lash of the whip nor intricate bondage. He snorted distain at needles and electrical play. He yawned at the idea of torture and anything to do with rubber or leather (or even latex) was enough to bring on drowsiness. Heaven only knows what he would have made of balloons and as for opera gloves? Well, I think by now you've got the idea. So what was his fix? How did this clearly focussed man express his kinky desires? Did he like to don a beekeepers hat and flippers and bathe in Jello or were his needs even darker, pushing the boundaries of good taste way beyond their limits? To be honest, it's difficult to say, you'll have to make up your own mind.

The combination of an attractive woman and a small plastic toy car in close proximity would be what set him a trembling. If the aforesaid woman then crushed the small vehicle into pieces underneath a booted foot Tarquin would be in seventh heaven. The more violently the crushing the greater the rush. If the vehicle was in motion at the time almost instant ecstasy was achieved.

Thus, at regular intervals, he'd emerge from Toys R Us with a bulging shopping bag and a determined look. He'd then make his way to his Mistress of choice, stopping only briefly to pick up his carefully constructed hand made ramp. Once ensconced in her playroom he would set up his inclined plane and calmly unpack his new doomed miniature automobile collection. What would be going through his mind at the time I'm sure we will never know.

Back down here on planet Earth what was going through my mind was, 'Don't wish too hard for what you want.' The irony of the statement I'd made to Jeanine previously echoed around my head as Domme Jackeline attached leather straps to my wrists. The commercial dungeon she'd booked for our session definitely looked the part and so did she. I was to discover she not only looked the part…she absolutely was the part. The mock provenance of our environment had been created with a sumptuous eye for detail. The walls appeared to be ancient stone with dim lamps affording a suitably low lighting. A pentangle on the floor gave an uncomfortable edge and the fully-fledged medieval rack some way behind me completed the superb set dressing. The icing on the cake was the dominatrix herself, stunning in a tight leather bodice and high black boots. She looked perfect.

The archetypal kink image is a beautiful dominatrix in a dungeon with a whip. Notwithstanding this I'd established, that with a few exceptions, the vast majority of kinksters, whilst adoring the vision, preferred the erotic side of kink. They wanted the full-blown lather clad Domme but they fantasised about a softer less cruel interaction. I'm generalising of course but most of my research seemed to confirm this. That was never my inclination. To me the image meant genuinely being whipped by a sadistic woman ostensibly for her own pleasure. As I've said, I'm not a masochist, but I enjoy the intellectual dynamics of submitting to someone worth submitting to. To put myself in their care, trusting that they will respect my limits whilst giving me 'the real thing'. I hated the pain Jackeline had heaped on me but I loved the fantasy of the dominance. To have one without the other was in my opinion 'cheating'. It had to be 'real' or it just wasn't, well, real.

From the day I'd seen Stacy as Mistress Alexandra I'd fantasised about this scenario. Would I be able to take it? Would I have the courage to see it through? What did single tail actually feel like? Endless questions and delicious anticipation. I was about to find out.

Once she'd attached the leather straps to my wrist she then clipped each one to an overhead bar, a bar she then winched up, stretching my arms apart and over my head. And with that she left the room. I stared at my naked frame in the nearby mirror suddenly feeling, in all honesty, rather silly. A wave of shame came over me. What the hell was I doing? I'd let this kink thing totally get out of hand. I half convinced myself I was going to call a stop to the session, feeling angry that I'd let myself end up here. I glared miserably at my reflection, my thoughts having totally yanked me out of my headspace. Fuck this for a game of soldiers, I was out of there!

Jackeline entered and I turned to vent my feelings "Be still," she commanded. Just looking at her in this environment scrambled my thoughts. I felt stupid and angry on the one hand and yet her persona made me comply. She stood directly behind me. I could see the two of us in the mirror. I felt strange. "I'm going to hood you," she stated. I once again snapped out of the zone. There was no way I was going to look like a gimp and I told her so in no uncertain terms. She ignored my petulant outburst "It's for safety," she soothed. Even I couldn't argue with that. I cringed as she put the tight leather hood over my face and laced it up behind my head. When she finished I glanced again at the mirror. What I saw genuinely shocked me. I was totally de humanised. I'd never felt this way before. It was almost as if her putting on the hood had taken away any last vestiges of power I had.

She slowly walked around in front of me. My emotions and thoughts were banging around in my head like the shiny sphere in a pinball machine. "Why are you here?" she asked. I couldn't think of an answer. She repeated the question. Humour, my first defence mechanism, came rampaging to the surface, "Because I've been a very naughty boy?" I said brightly and laughed. A hint of a smile passed her lips and she walked behind me. "I'm going to start you off with a flogger," she said, "That'll warm you up for the single tail." I mentally yawned. A flogger? Yeah, sure they're thuddy but they weren't serious pain. I'd always eschewed them as they bored me but, who was I to argue?

She stood back and raised the implement above her head, and brought it down over my back so hard I saw stars...literally. I went to say something but before I could open my mouth stroke two fell equally as hard. Jesus. Then came the third and then the forth. By now I wasn't thinking of complaining, I was just desperately trying to hold on. No one had ever hit me like this before, not even close and certainly not with a flogger. The onslaught continued. I was grunting at every stroke. Within five minutes the grunts had turned to yells. I couldn't believe how severely she was flaying me. Any thoughts, erotic or otherwise, regarding the presence of a beautiful leather clad dominatrix were long gone. All I was aware of was the beating and trying to get through it. I'd wanted real and as I reflected whilst trying to catch my breath between strokes, that was what I was getting. And this was just the warm up. I cursed myself for my stupidly. Why did I think this was going to be fun? I could stop it with a word.

But I didn't. Even though Jackeline was being paid to do this I allowed myself the fantasy of thinking she'd want me to take it. The intensity of her assault broke down my mental boundaries. I was living in world of pain and the flogging was all there was. I just knew I'd get through it if I could just take the next stroke and then next. I wouldn't wimp out, I just wouldn't. And then it was over. "Are you there?" she inquired. I couldn't speak. She walked around in front of me "Are you there?" she repeated. I nodded. "Tell Me," she said. "I'm here," I whispered, "Just."

She held a small bottle of water to my lips and I gratefully gulped down its contents. I started babbling about never having been hit so hard but she put her finger to my lips "Quiet," she said, "Enjoy the endorphins." Enjoy the endorphins? My back was ablaze! A moment later she was back, single tail in hand. I knew I was in trouble when for the first time ever she gave me a safe word and a further one to indicate when she should ease up. I agreed to the first one but refused the second. We were either going to do this properly or not at all. And of course it's always easy to be brave before the event.

Once again she stood behind me. Being the veteran I was I knew what to expect. A few taps to mark the distance and then a variety of different throws gently building me up to a final onslaught. And so it began. One light tap to mark the distance and then WHAM a napalm stroke that had me yelling at the top of my voice. I wasn't doing the single tailing, Jackeline was and she demonstrably wasn't me. I twisted round to complain when stroke two hit the target and I yelled blue murder trying to process the pain. Strokes three and four were lighter and

I hardly felt stroke five. Stroke six exploded through my consciousness like double-barrelled shotgun blast. A slash of unbearable white pain cut through me from shoulder to waist. I almost screamed. This was a real as it got. She eased off slightly, allowing me to almost gain some form of composure before unloading three back-to-back strokes which made me yell so loudly I thought I'd ruptured my voice box. I glimpsed my tormentor in the mirror, her face was calm and composed and totally unaffected by my distress. Perfect.

And so it continued for the next twenty minutes. My back was beyond raw. For every two or three almost bearable strokes there would an unbearable one. There were no exotic throws from Domme Jackeline, this was a full-blown balls to the wall whipping. When being caned one knows approximately where the strike is coming and roughly what it will feel like so one can almost prepare for it. With single tail none of this information is available making preparation impossible. Additionally, being hit across the back gives a totally different range of sensations, which in turn gives rise to a completely different set of physiological reactions. The reality of this was being brought home to me in a very real and dramatic way. I was aware, to my horror, that the intense pain was bringing me close to tears. A scenario which I'd never even begun to consider as a possibility. I swallowed and dug deep. Anything to avoid that level of shame. I'd never bottomed at this level before and it was taking me to somewhere I'd never been. A blinding stroke across the centre of my back was the tipping point and, mortally embarrassed, I felt my eyes moisten. Within a minute there was no hiding it, I was very obviously crying and each stroke made it worse. And Jackeline's reaction? She didn't back off for a moment, not for a bloody second. I had final confirmation of what had been so amply demonstrated in my past encounters with her. This woman was the genuine article. Ruthless and pitiless. A true dominatrix, not a kitten in leather.

She continued whipping me mercilessly until my knees started to go and I shouted, "STOP." She ceased immediately.

At this point I was reminded of my own experiences when I'd taken someone this far and indeed some of Stacy's wise words from the past regarding heavy play. You bring someone down gently and soothingly. 'Aftercare' was the word used. The blubbering mess that was me certainly needed it. My tormentor strode over and I waited for the affectionate hug and the murmurs of "Well done." She put her hand under my chin and fixed me with a stare. She then jerked my head up and hissed, "Compose yourself!" And that was it.

Well, I certainly couldn't complain about a lack of authenticity.

Chapter Fifteen

Full Circle

There was a living legend that lurked in the steamy far-flung reaches of exotic Asia. Even Penny spoke in hushed reverential tones when referring to 'Awesome Anouk', a woman of such commitment to the cause, she'd sent twenty year hardened topping veterans away with their heads hung in shame. In the teeming metropolis of Hong Kong Anouk dismissed the endeavours of one would be disciplinarian after another with a sharp tongue and an apparently inexhaustible appetite for punishment. Even 'Fanatical Frank', a man so tough he could break Tonka Toys (when he wasn't shaving his testicles with a blunt cut throat razor) had been branded 'Uninteresting' and 'a pathetic novice'. "Jesus mate," he reported, "She made me feel like a fucking drongo." All this attitude was apparently encompassed in a mere one hundred and five pounds of Chinese sveltness with a simply gorgeous face. She'd never ever safe worded and when being punished continually punctuated the session with sneers and disparaging remarks directed at her tops inadequacies. Penny, who was the ultimate spanking matchmaking master, had sent her failure after failure. All efforts to quench this five-foot dynamos appetites had crashed and burned. Penny heard of a planned business trip I had to the Orient and immediately pounced. Intrigued, I acquiesced to have my name put forward under certain conditions. Clearly this supplicant needed some unique handling.

I thought about strategy and tactics and outlined my plan to Penny. She giggled in agreement. Following my instructions she called Hong Kong and relayed the following. "Look Anouk, there is one other person I know but I've held off until now because quite honestly you'd find him way too severe. He's probably not for you." Needless to say Anouk had bitten and bitten extremely hard. Penny continued, "He's very difficult to get to see and he's unbelievably fussy who he plays with. I do know though that he's coming to Hong Kong soon. Perhaps if you write him a really nice note I'll put a good word in for you as well and see if I can persuade him to see you." Penny had followed my words to the letter and already Anouk was knocked a little off her stride. She'd been used to gushing letters of introduction from previous spankers. She'd never had to make the first move herself. Sure enough an email arrived shortly afterwards.

I read the epistle with a quiet smile. She'd been very polite and respectful and earnestly requested I take her seriously as a play partner. Penny laughed her head off when I read the letter back to her. She'd never known Anouk like this. I replied three days later in a brusque and no nonsense fashion. I criticised her English, bemoaned the quality of her syntax and questioned her spanking credentials. I concluded in my communication that the quality of her note indicated she wasn't worthy of my attention however, solely as favour to Penny, I'd agree to beat her. I confirmed the date I would meet her some four weeks hence and told her to come to my hotel room at 8.15pm sharp, indicating if she was so much as five minutes late I wouldn't see her. Furthermore, I told her there would be no further correspondence between us until that day. I finished by saying if she concurred with this then I wanted a mail back immediately simply saying. "Yes Sir, I understand" and nothing else. I received the required note a mere ten minutes after I'd sent mine. Huge fun. OK then, I'd talked the talk. I was now going to have to walk the walk. Penny reported the following day she'd received a mail from Anouk saying, "You know, this guy gives me butterflies." I'd got her and we hadn't even met. Perfect.

Upon my arrival in the Hong Kong hotel it was late and I was exhausted from the long and totally wretched flight, a flight enhanced not one bit by the fact I was sat next to a terminally verbose American Football Player. He was to convivial conversation what the British are to cosmetic dentistry. Evidently famous at home, I'd never heard of him and his efforts to engage me in conversation made me seriously consider lobbying congress for his compulsory euthanasia. He had the sort of a head that looked like it had spent far too much time in a crash helmet and he droned interminably on about the pressure and his stats, evidently having 'rushed' an awful lot that season. Unimpressed I observed I'd 'rush' pretty smartly too if I was being chased down by two hundred and fifty pound Neanderthals in full body amour intent on maiming me for life. I'm sure in a bar full of doe eyed supplicants he's as popular as porn in a prison library but I'm a tougher audience. I s'pose it's not his fault he didn't know I was raised by wolves. The fact that this guy was very good looking and in great shape (and younger than me) has nothing to do with this rant OK?

The passenger on the other side of me was no better. My first guess would have been she was a test pilot at a broomstick factory. A Bavarian by birth she aggressively engaged me in conversation despite my non-committal grunts to her opening gambits. Eventually she broke me down and the subject of 'The British' came up. A subject I was relatively unwilling to discuss with a German...way too much material you know? Coming from a race with no personality at all I was aghast she would leave himself so open but, as ever, I bit my tongue and ground my teeth whilst fervently wishing her an immediate case of terminal deep vein thrombosis.

At the hotel, headache haunted and jet lagged, I went directly to my room, undressed and crashed immediately. I must reveal (for reasons you'll see later) that I sleep au naturel. I then woke up with a pressing need for a glass of water. As the room was in total darkness and I was so tired, I got out of bed without even bothering to open my eyes. I fumbled around and found the bathroom door and felt around for the washbasin. After stumbling around for about fifteen seconds it occurred to me that this seemed to be a much bigger bathroom than I remembered it to be. I opened my eyes to discover I was in the corridor outside my room...stark naked! In abject horror I turned immediately around to see my bedroom door slowly swinging shut. With an Olympian lunge I managed to grab the handle before it clicked shut. It took a full half hour for my heart rate to subside. Next morning I noted there were no house phones on my floor...not even a plant to hide my modesty. I would have had to go down to reception to request another key...Oh God...even as I type this my blood is running cold!

"This," I said, whilst brandishing a ferocious paddle, "Is 'Old Faithful'." Anouk, dressed solely in white vest, white panties and white socks, regarded it cautiously with her fabulous almond eyes. "I use it to keep my supplicants attention focussed," I spoke slowly. "If you fail to follow my instructions immediately you'll get a stroke. If you deviate from my directives you'll get a stroke. If you move without being told to you'll get a stroke, If you speak without being spoken to you'll get a stroke. Do I make myself absolutely clear?" She nodded.

"Dear me," I admonished, "I think you mean 'Yes Sir'. That calls for a stroke. Bend over and put your hands on your knees." With a hint of resignation she did so and I administered a swat which you could have heard on the far side of Kowloon Harbour. She grunted slightly and stood up. "I don't recall telling you to stand up," I admonished, "That's another demerit. Please resume the position." As she bent over I continued my dialogue, "I didn't fully explain how 'old faithful' works. Please forgive my forgetfulness. Each time you earn a demerit I add an extra stroke. This means I've now got to give you two. And we haven't even started your actual punishment yet." I then gave her two swats that the England Cricket Captain would have been proud of. This time she stayed in position. I was impressed. I knew from grim personal experience that this paddle hurt like buggery. Not that I've experienced buggery you understand, it's merely a figure of speech.

I looked down at the delightful little package in front of me. "I've always felt," I murmured, "That young ladies were born with their brains in their bottoms. That being the case they need to be beaten up to their heads. Wouldn't you agree Anouk? She gave a delicious little giggle. "Wrong answer," I snapped, "That's three more." A three that I delivered with a no nonsense alacrity. I got a squeak out of her on stroke three. "You may stand," I informed her.

She stood as instructed. Legs together, hands by her sides and head lowered. "Right," I continued, "I want you to go into the bathroom. Remove your panties and run them under the tap until they're soaked through. Then put them on again and return to me." "What?" she said incredulously. I shook my head sadly. "That's the wrong answer Anouk. Please resume the position. We're up to four now I believe?" Her face was a picture and it was all I could do not to laugh. She suddenly realised what she had got herself into and there was no hiding place.

Anouks appetite for discipline was unbelievable. For almost an hour I beat her relentlessly, she grunting and squeaking occasionally whilst sweat literally flowed down my face. The culmination was a thundering three hundred stoke caning. The last fifty of which were as hard as I could manage whilst still maintaining accuracy. When I finished we were both exhausted. "That," I admitted, "Was the hardest session I've ever administered. Unbelievable. Well done!" She lay on the bed with a dreamy look on her exquisite face. "Wonderful," she gasped, "That was just wonderful."

A while later we were enjoying nibbles at the hotel bar. Anouk, I discovered, was not only beautiful but also (excuse the expression) 'whip smart' and, as seems to be the case with all quality players, possessed of an outstanding sense of humour. Twenty minutes into our most enjoyable post session chat she said, "When we've finished our drinks can we do it again?" She was serious. I was stunned. This girl was beyond hard core. An idea germinated in my mind. "I'm not going to do that again," I counselled, "Your butts taken enough punishment and if I do any more the skins going to break and you won't thank me for that." "Ohh, you mean blood?" she enthused, "I don't mind." Dear me. "I do I'm afraid," I replied, "But I've got an idea."

Forty minutes later, back in the hotel room, Anouk was handling my single tail whip like a newborn kitten. "Oh my God," she said, "I've always dreamed of something like this." Her dreams came true shortly afterwards. What she took from the whip was amazing and she adored it. To her shock and amazement she finally safe worded for the first time ever. With the single tail they always do…eventually.

Anouks squeals were compounded by Penney's yelps in Boston, Jeanine's gasps in Chicago and Hannah's tears the day after I arrived back home in New York. An awful lot of kink in a very short timescale but still fun. On the plane home I reflected I'd now come full circle and finally attained that which I'd set out to achieve. I now knew I could enjoy my 'dark passenger' whenever I so wished and subsequently found once again that the actual need to do so is tempered by such knowledge. I'd initially arrived in the city hungry for that which I craved and once the floodgates had finally opened I can be legitimately accused of an element of gluttony. Gluttony is regarded as a bad thing but (excuse the oxymoron) in moderation it can serve its purpose. Without that gluttony I would never have met some the wonderful friends I have now. Seeing that my appetites have been my constant companion since I was eight years old I cannot envisage them leaving me now. I know them to be part of who I am and I'm more than comfortable with that. What I sometimes cursed about myself I now embrace as I once did previously.

Through my baptism of fire to re kindle this aspect of my life I genuinely went on a journey, a great deal of which I've detailed in this account. It was occasionally depressing and sometimes de motivating but also sporadically exhilarating, funny, fulfilling, erotic and never ever boring. I don't regret a single moment. Actually, that's a lie but fortunately it's good one. For the most part it was invigorating and it still is but it's now no longer a journey. I've arrived at my intended destination.

I still very occasionally deal with Trust Fund Trudy for hard cash, though thankfully poor Gerrys now long gone. Pernicious Penny is as active as ever as a spanking doyen in Boston and if ever I'm in Massachusetts I see to her needs. Juiced Jeanine visits Manhattan a couple of times a year and fesses up enthusiastically. Dear Committed Chloe has all but vanished from the fray but Hard Core Hanna still pops her head over the parapet every now and again. Single Tail Celestes now married (thankfully to a spanking fanatic) but sends me the odd mad amusing email and I still very occasionally scratch my own itch. I've re found the wonderful balance that I had back in the day. Vanilla and kink now co exist peaceably. And Awesome Anouk? I'm currently trying to arrange a trans continental meet between her and Domme Jackeline. A true 'Clash of the Titans'! That's one I'm really looking forward to seeing and I've pre booked my front row seat.

Of course vanilla is no less thrilling than kink and fraught with its own range of problems and mysteries. Not for me of course, I'm naturally talking generally. Given time however these problems can be overcome and the mysteries err demystified. I eventually found out for example that women fake orgasms because men fake foreplay. Not something which I can be accused of, though in my callow youth I certainly lacked an edge of sophistication in such matters. I confess my idea of safe sex was a padded headboard. Expectations too are sometimes unreasonably high. I recall nudging a recent beau suggestively inquiring, "Fancy a quickie?" for her to reply, "As opposed to what?" And lets not even go into the fact that unbelievably there are still those who believe in the ever persistent myth of the female orgasm. I'll say no more for now. Suffice to say that both worlds have their challenges and far-flung journeys within each are equally stimulating.

Concerning journeys, and I apologise for the tenuous link, my next business trip was to the Netherlands. Amsterdam to be precise, where I had two memorable episodes. After finishing my business affairs I stumbled across the city's apparently well known (but not to me) 'Museum of Torture', a few blocks from my hotel. I naturally couldn't resist a quick peek. I staggered out an hour later having been put off kink for life, or at least for the next thirty minutes.

My second episode was infinitely more pleasurable. I paid a visit to an old friend. The friend concerned was a retired woman who had moved to the city some years previously. We stay in touch as we used have the most unusual relationship and hilarious conversations back in the day. Now, at sixty-nine she is still the epitome of the word 'Different'. She wears tie dies, smokes grass in quantities that defy the imagination and she's a Hendrix freak, all of which meets with my wholehearted approval. She also refuses to upgrade from her vinyl record collection. She calls 'CDs 'new fangled' and as for the Internet, she describes it as a 'fad for the bored and those that lack imagination or who cant be bothered to go to libraries'. Truly a unique character, stepping into her apartment is like going back to the 1960s when even I wasn't yet a teenager.

She's a strict vegetarian and cooks up the most amazing concoctions. I just have to ensure she doesn't add any of her 'special spices' which she is inclined to do. She has waist length grey hair which she refuses to dye, has a yoga workout regime which puts most instructors to shame, and, delightfully, has a very long trail of totally devoted male admirers whom she sees regularly. I am not one of that long trail for the simple reason I'm way too old for her! On the seldom occasions we get together, we eat well and talk of our adventures, though she is a lot more explicit than I. She takes delight in being totally

outrageous, outspoken, unconventional and deeply spiritual…
truly one in a million.

"So," she said, "How is New York?"

It's always good to catch up with Stacy again.

About the Author

John Smith

John Smith, it must be said, is less impressive in the flesh than you would probably imagine. A fey countenance combined unattractively with an irrational intolerance are his first lines of defence in his continuing epic struggle with humanity.

When not indulging in his kink persuasions he spends his time attempting to earn a living traveling the Globe in search of foreigners unwise enough to pay money for his consulting acumen. He can most often be spotted at airports, gazing fretfully for signs to the business class lounge, whilst making legion efforts to avoid eye contact with anyone at all. Further clues as to his identity are a weary disposition together with a feigned genial diffidence, both of which unexpectedly disguise a direct manner that few airline staff are prepared to tolerate.

He is also recognizable by the lack of an endearing smile or a disarming candor. Easily startled, he should be approached only with great caution. The current advice concerning a conversation opener are a) the soothing offer of an immediate upgrade to first class or b) at the very least, fine cuisine.

John, to his immense dismay and horror, is nudging his half-century and currently lives with an enforced and uneasy tranquility somewhere in Manhattan.

Lightning Source UK Ltd.
Milton Keynes UK
22 November 2010

9 781610 981101